TROPICAL FRUIT *of* THAILAND

Desmond Tate

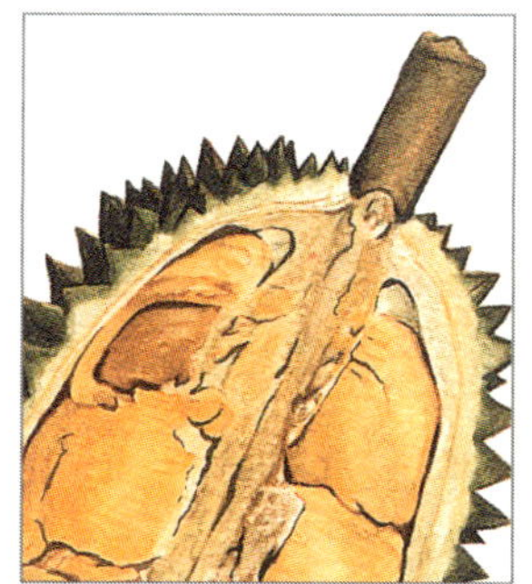

Editor: *Amita Sarwal*
Designer: *Norreha Bt. Sayuti*

Illustrators: *Bruce Granquist*
Anuar Bin Abdul Rahim

Agus Saramulloh
Anuwar Firdaus
Atang Fachruroji
Duky Noermalla
Iman Sudjudi
Komang Agus Bagiada
Mubinas Hanafi
Neddi Supriadi
Nengah Nurenten
Soni Mandriana
Susilowati
Tata Sugiarta
Ujang Suherman
Yoga Kusuma

Photographs courtesy of EDM Archives and Tara Sosrowardoyo

Although the author and publisher have tried to make the information as accurate as possible, they accept no responsibility for any injury or other adverse effects sustained by any person using this book or as a consequence of the information in it.

ISBN: 981-4068-01-2

Published and Distributed in Thailand by:
Asia Books Co. Ltd
5 Sukhumvit Road Soi 61
Bangkok 10110, Thailand
P.O. Box 40
Tel: (66 2) 714-0740-2 ext. 221-223
Fax: (66 2) 381-1621, 391-2277
E-mail: customer_serv@asiabooks.co.th

Printed by Tien Wah Press, Singapore

TROPICAL FRUIT *of* THAILAND

Desmond Tate

ASIA BOOKS

C O N T E N T S

Tropical Fruit

Celebrating Nature's Bounty

Neatly and artistically cut fresh fruit are displayed in a glass case at a fruit vendor's stall.

Fruit brings to mind the succulent product of a tree or plant, most satisfying to the palate and, to an extent, associated with affluence, luxury and a touch of decadence. Tropical fruit, specifically, is reinforced with a hint of the exotic.

The word 'tropical' itself is heavily laden with a sense of abundance and profusion. The lands of the tropics girdle the earth at its widest point, forming a region spanning three continents and possessing in common, despite great differences in local conditions, a regime whose perennial heat and abundant rainfall create a luxuriant plant life and produce a wide diversity of remarkable fruits. At the same time, while temperatures are relatively even and rainfall ample, there are also the cooler hills and plateaus, isolated drier zones and contrasts between poor and fertile soils which permit considerable variation in tree and plant types. In brief, the tropics make for a fruit aficionado's paradise.

A painting showing a Javanese hawker selling fresh fruit juice, circa 19th century.

The fruit diaspora

Today, most tropical fruits are no longer confined to their original home-lands but are to be found in all parts of the tropical world. The principal donors in this respect have been the tropical Americas. The chiku, cinchona, cocoa, guava, papaya, pineapple and soursop, now thoroughly at home in other parts of the tropical world, are all migrants from South and Central America or the West Indies. The jackfruit and water apple, also widespread throughout the tropics, came originally from India; the pomegranate is the gift of Persia; the watermelon, a product of tropical Africa (as is also the oil palm); and the coconut started off (probably) somewhere in the South Pacific. Southeast Asia, on the other hand, despite the great abundance and diversity of its own indigenous fruits, has been less generous. This is mainly because some of its best fruits—the durian, mangosteen and rambutan—do not travel well. But the world must be grateful to that corner of the globe too for the banana, lime, pomelo and carambola (star fruit).

The chief method for the dissemination of these fruits from their homelands has been via the trade routes, by sea and overland. The principal disseminators have been the Spaniards and the Portuguese. These advance guards of European imperialism, who first scoured the world's oceans in the 16th century, wasted no time in introducing the new commodities they 'discovered' in the Americas and elsewhere to Europe and other parts of the world. The Spaniards introduced the fruits of Mexico, Brazil and the West Indies via Manila and the Philippines to the rest of Southeast Asia and beyond. Likewise, the Portuguese, whose 16th-century maritime empire was still more far-flung, brought American produce to Southeast Asia via Melaka in the Malay Peninsula; to India via Goa; and to west and east Africa. Yet long before this, traders and seafarers in the Indian Ocean such as the Tamils of southern India, the Malays and the Arabs had already made their mark. The fruits of India arrived in Southeast Asia generations before the Christian era, AD 1, carried by merchants from Coromandel and Malabar, while the coconut probably transported itself to the Moluccas, borne by sea currents from Polynesia at the very dawn of history.

A new dimension to the globalisation of tropical fruits came with the Industrial Revolution and the introduction of machines, in particular with the start of the fruit canning industry in the 19th century. One of the first

Stamps of Singapore and Thailand showing the jackfruit and rambutan.

Fruit, as a still life form on canvas, has inspired artists since early times. Below is an artist's impression—Banana Tree by M. Carsten.

Fresh passion fruit juice is very popular in Southeast Asia. The label on the bottle mentions the fruit's high vitamin C content.

and main beneficiaries was the pineapple, now to be found in its canned form all over the world. Other more exotic fruits which once could never have expected to travel anywhere beyond their homeland have now become established on the world market. One leading example is the lychee of China which entered this domain only after World War II.

The food equation

The prime use of fruit always has been, and remains, a part of our diet, although some fruits (such as the oil palm fruit) are not edible. At various periods, local fruits became transformed into symbols of luxury when they arrived on the tables of the rich and mighty in foreign climes. The pomegranate had won the approval of the patricians of Rome before the birth of Jesus Christ. In the 8th century, the Tang Emperor Hsuan Tsung was prepared to bankrupt his empire in an attempt to win the heart of the beautiful princess Yang Kuei Fei with a supply of lychees. The pineapple was held the aristocrat of all fruits by the 16th-century monarchs of Spain. In the century which followed, the preoccupation of the Malay sultan of Johor with the jackfruit cost him his life and ended a dynasty. In the 19th century, Victoria, the great White Queen-Empress, offered a reward to anyone who successfully imported the mangosteen into the British Isles. Even today the avocado is regarded as a symbol of elegance and affluence.

The fruit of the tropics vary greatly in the range of their applications in the kitchen and in the nature of their preparation for various dishes at the table. It might be argued that the best fruit are those which are simply consumed as such, straight from the tree or plant. No one would dispute the standing of the mango or mangosteen, the lychee, rambutan or papaya in this respect, nor—in the case of those who have acquired the taste—the durian either. In general, tropical fruit perform best as rich and tasty desserts and refreshing drinks. A good number of them, such as the guava and the chempedak, also form great standbys for pickles and preserves, while yet

Linschoten, during his travels in Southeast Asia, mentions in his book Itinerario, Voyage ofte Schipvaert (1596) that the semi-translucent starfruit can be eaten green as a vegetable, and when ripe as a dessert. He further adds that in China it was known as a 'foreign peach'.

others fit easily into salads, serve as flavourings in ice cream and make excellent sauces to go with meat, poultry and fish. And certain among them—of which the pineapple, banana and coconut are outstanding examples—simply possess an amazing versatility and turn up in all manner of different culinary combinations, besides having served for centuries as established ingredients in staple regional curries and savouries.

The attractive salmon-pink, juicy segments of the pomelo are visible once the thick rind is removed.

However, in its natural setting the average tropical fruit simply functions as a welcome addition to the local fare. Some of them (notably the breadfruit and certain palm fruit including, again, the coconut), because of their ease of cultivation, high nutritional value and versatility, have always been integral elements in the diets of local communities, particularly those who live at subsistence level.

The versatility of fruit

Fruit and the other components of their native plant—trunk, stem, sap, leaves, fibres—have a wide range of practical applications. The jack of all trades in this respect is the coconut, which is truly multipurpose and can virtually provide human beings with all their basic needs. Other fruits offer applications that range from the caulking of boats to the manufacture of rope (Manila hemp) and the fashioning of kitchen utensils.

The alternate applications and uses of tropical fruit reflect a fascinating blend of traditional wisdom and experience combined with modern research. Many of the conventional applications of these fruit have been

Bananas are one of the best examples of plants that travel well and thrive anywhere in the tropics. For this reason it is hard to determine their provenance. It is established that bananas were introduced to the New World by the Spanish who brought them from the Canary Islands.

superseded by the advances of science, although as far as their medicinal properties are concerned, there is still plenty of scope. The thrust of modern technology and research has lain first and foremost in achieving better yields in terms of quality and quantity, as well as finding new industrial uses for them. The result has been that some tropical fruit have acquired a usefulness and purpose which they had not known previously.

The prime example of this is the oil palm which was virtually functionless until the early years of the 20th century when, as a result of a series of scientific breakthroughs, vegetable oils became commercially viable. The oil palm now thrives very profitably wherever it is cultivated—in West Africa, South America or Southeast Asia—because the oil from its fruit has become one of the most successful of the marketable natural vegetable oils. In terms of export value, it is the most important commercial export crop of both Indonesia and Malaysia. Furthermore, the oil palm has other uses: the shells can be used in road building, kernels as fuel in oil palm mills, empty fruit bunches as fertilizer, palm fronds and palm kernel cake as cattle feed, and tree trunks for making panel board for the construction industry.

Nothing can compare with a basketful of fresh fruit—untouched by preservatives and the canning industry.

Fruit in this book

The fruit featured in this book have been selected primarily because of their flavour, but also as much for their idiosyncrasies and historical and medicinal significance. Indeed, while most of the fruits will be familiar and are commonly found on tables worldwide, there are those which are quite unlikely to make it onto the restaurant menu, whether because of their inability to travel or perhaps because theirs is an acquired taste.

Nevertheless, the presentation is not entirely without design. Basic information on each fruit is given, which is consistent with the available data and the appropriate context. At the same time, general descriptions aim to provide facts about the fruit in question and its salient characteristics—but in not too regimented a fashion. Some fruits warrant longer descriptions than others. The illustrations, which have been carefully drawn so as to be as accurate and true to life as possible, complement the text beautifully. The recipes for many of the fruits in this collection originated from some of the best five-star kitchens in the region—the leading hotels and resorts. These are basically for those fruits that lend themselves to cooking. Since this is not a cookery book, the recipes that have been provided are there more as an indication of their exotic possibilities than anything else.

This book is written in the hope that its contents will inspire the curious to explore a little further at their leisure into what is surely a vast and appetizing field—and perhaps experiment with the recipes.

Banana trees are described here as 'Indian figs'. This painting is from 'Mr John Nieuhoff's Remarkable Voyages and Travels into ye best Provinces in ye West and East Indies', published in A Collection of Voyages & Travels, compiled by Awnsham Churchill, London (1732).

DIMENSIONS:

tree:
height: up to 12–13 m

fruit:
diameter: 5-12.5 cm
weight: 1-2.5 kg

SEASON:
dry season

PROPAGATION:
seeds

CULINARY USES:
eaten fresh; also prepared as a syrup

OTHER USES:
traditional medicine (juice and leaves)

Aegle marmelos

BAEL FRUIT

(Thai name: *ma-toom*)

Origin:
India

Distribution:
Indian subcontinent, north Luzon (Philippines), Thailand, Java and the Malay Peninsula

Varieties:
Wild (small), cultivated (larger size)

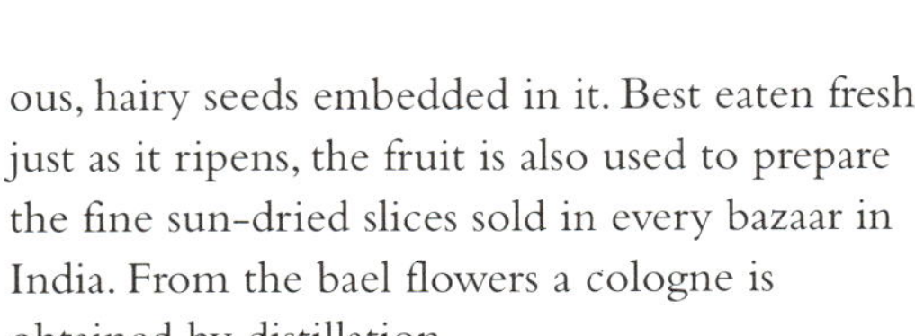

Artists add the fruit's pulp to their watercolours. It is also known to be applied as a protective coating on paintings.

Pill- and snuff-boxes, sometimes embellished with gold or silver, are crafted from the hard outer shell of the fruit.

In rural areas, the fruit, which has binding qualities, is mixed with lime plaster for water-proofing wells and is added to cement for building walls in villages.

The bael fruit tree with its highly fragrant flowers is commonly grown in India, and can be found near most temples as it is dedicated to Lord Siva and its leaves are used in religious ceremonies. The tree is also regarded as sacred in Indonesia and Malaysia, to where it was probably brought by Hindu traders.

The common name of the tree is derived from Sanskrit. It is known as *bael, bel* or *sirphal* in India; *matum* in Thailand; *maja* in Malaysia and Indonesia; Bengal quince in Australia; *oranger du Malabar* in French and as *marmelos* in Portuguese. The Javanese name, *majapahit*—*maja* being a corruption of the Sanskrit *maha* meaning great—is an indication of the veneration in which it is held. *Pahit* means bitter, a reminder of its astringent taste. Hence, the significance of the name of the great 14th-century Javanese empire of Majapahit, which was derived from this tree.

Bael fruit, which belongs to the same family as the orange, has a thin hard woody shell, yellow when ripe. The pulp of the fruit is orange-coloured, with numerous, hairy seeds embedded in it. Best eaten fresh just as it ripens, the fruit is also used to prepare the fine sun-dried slices sold in every bazaar in India. From the bael flowers a cologne is obtained by distillation.

However, the bael fruit's claim to fame rests most on its medicinal properties. Its high tannin content makes it, as the Portuguese discovered, an effective cure for dysentery and cholera, as well as a remedy for other ailments. A sherbet is made from the pulp, which tastes like marmalade, and is taken for its mild laxative and digestive effects.

A decoction of the unripe fruit with ginger and fennel is said to be effective for the treatment of haemorrhoids. The pulp is also used in the treatment of leucoderma.

The fruit has detergent-like qualities and is often used as a soap substitute and for washing clothes in some rural areas.

The rind of the unripe fruit is used in tanning and also yields a yellow dye for the calico and silk textiles industry.

DIMENSIONS:
tree:
10–15 m
nut:
length: 3 cm
diameter: 2.5 cm

apple:
length: 10–20 cm
diameter: 4–8 cm

MATURITY
3–5 years

PROPAGATION:
seeds; grafting

CULINARY USES:
nut: snack, in sweet and savoury dishes
apple: drinks, candied

OTHER USES:
timber; gum; lubricant, insecticide (shell oil); ink (apple juice); skincare products (apple); traditional medicine

The nut, the true fruit, develops from the flower. Only when the nut is fully grown, but not yet ripe, does the cashew apple swell up.

Anacardium occidentale

CASHEW

Origin:
Brazil

Distribution:
South and Central America, East Africa, Asia

Varieties:
None

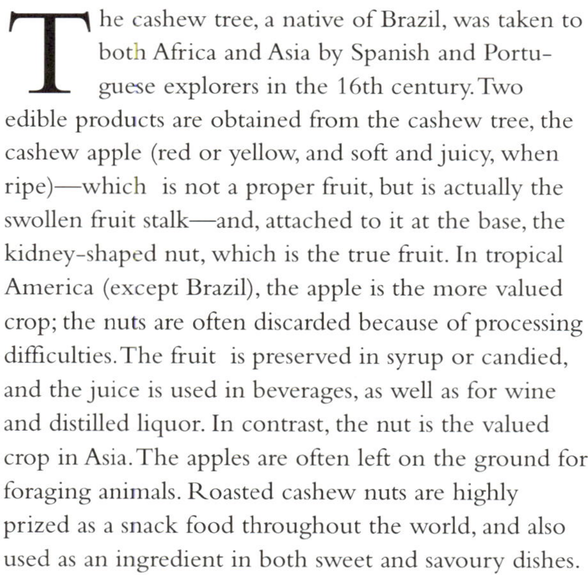

The cashew tree, a native of Brazil, was taken to both Africa and Asia by Spanish and Portuguese explorers in the 16th century. Two edible products are obtained from the cashew tree, the cashew apple (red or yellow, and soft and juicy, when ripe)—which is not a proper fruit, but is actually the swollen fruit stalk—and, attached to it at the base, the kidney-shaped nut, which is the true fruit. In tropical America (except Brazil), the apple is the more valued crop; the nuts are often discarded because of processing difficulties. The fruit is preserved in syrup or candied, and the juice is used in beverages, as well as for wine and distilled liquor. In contrast, the nut is the valued crop in Asia. The apples are often left on the ground for foraging animals. Roasted cashew nuts are highly prized as a snack food throughout the world, and also used as an ingredient in both sweet and savoury dishes.

The processing of cashew must be done with care as they have two shells—an outer hard one and an inner papery one—and the space between the two contains a caustic, inflammable oil. Roasting the nuts over an open fire in the traditional manner can result in the inhalation of poisonous fumes. Modern methods are much safer—as the nuts are roasted, shelled, peeled and graded mechanically, and the valuable oil can be collected.

Every part of the cashew tree has multiple uses. The timber is used in furniture making, boat building and for charcoal. The bark is used in tanning as well as medicinally. The clear gum tapped from the bark is used by the pharmaceutical industry. Uses of the nut shell oil include as lubricant, as insecticide, and in plastic production. Edible oil can be extracted from the nuts. The cashew apple juice and skin are used in skincare products and the juice, which turns black on exposure to air, also provides an indelible ink.

The leaves, bark and apple are used in traditional medicine. Cashew apple juice, containing vitamin C, is an effective anti-scurvy agent. It is also used to treat tonsillitis in Indonesia, dysentery in the Philippines, and influenza in the Amazon. The apple is also believed to have antitumour properties. In Malaysia, a decoction of the bark is used to treat diarrhoea and thrush, and a leaf decoction is gargled for a sore throat. In Indonesia, old leaves are applied to skin afflictions and burns. Cubans use the resin for treating colds.

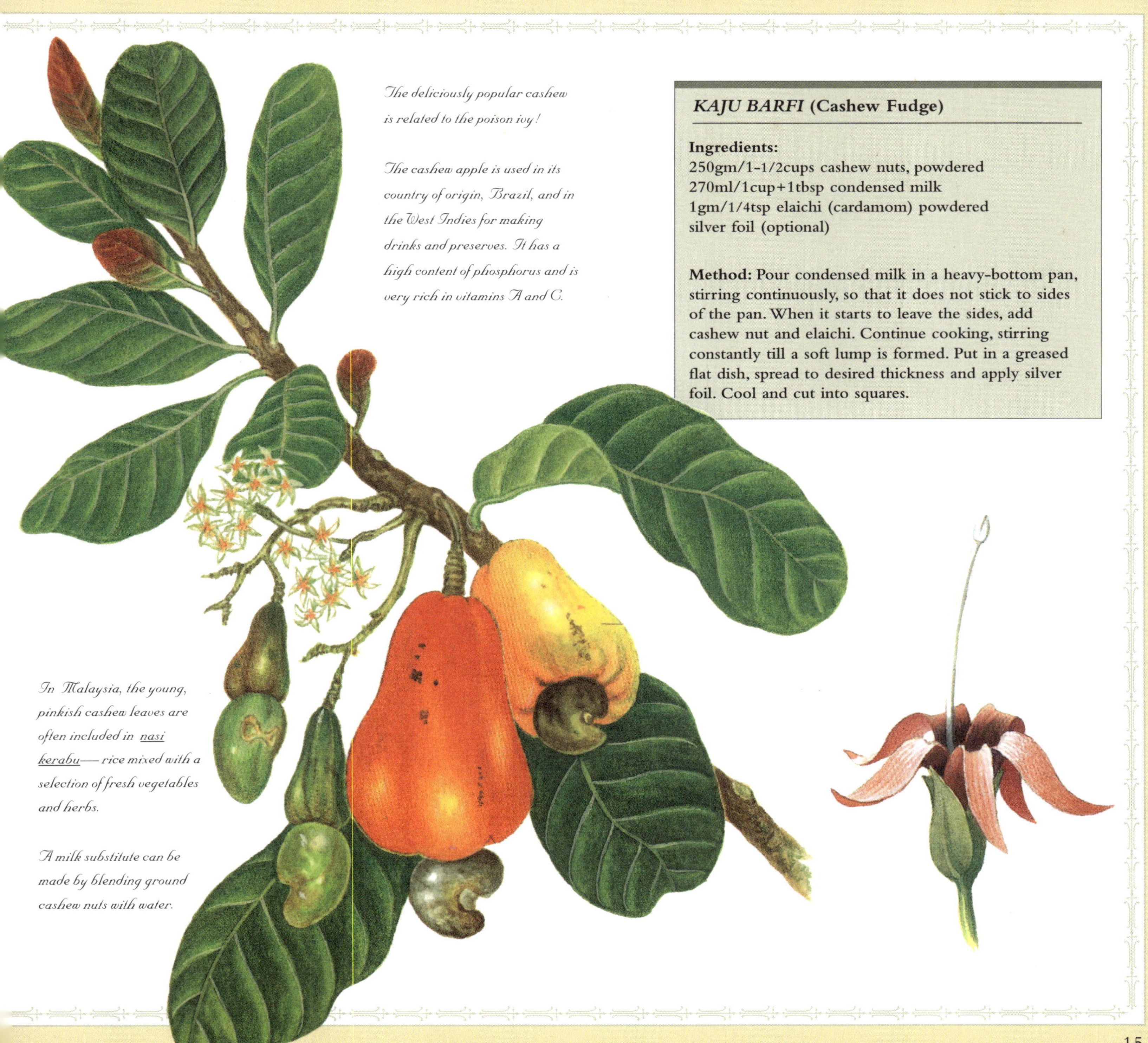

The deliciously popular cashew is related to the poison ivy!

The cashew apple is used in its country of origin, Brazil, and in the West Indies for making drinks and preserves. It has a high content of phosphorus and is very rich in vitamins A and C.

KAJU BARFI (Cashew Fudge)

Ingredients:
250gm/1-1/2cups cashew nuts, powdered
270ml/1cup+1tbsp condensed milk
1gm/1/4tsp elaichi (cardamom) powdered
silver foil (optional)

Method: Pour condensed milk in a heavy-bottom pan, stirring continuously, so that it does not stick to sides of the pan. When it starts to leave the sides, add cashew nut and elaichi. Continue cooking, stirring constantly till a soft lump is formed. Put in a greased flat dish, spread to desired thickness and apply silver foil. Cool and cut into squares.

In Malaysia, the young, pinkish cashew leaves are often included in nasi kerabu— rice mixed with a selection of fresh vegetables and herbs.

A milk substitute can be made by blending ground cashew nuts with water.

DIMENSIONS:

fruit:
diameter: 20–30 cm
length: 20–30 cm
weight: 0.6–2 kg

MATURITY:
12–14 months

PRODUCTIVITY:
12–30 months

SEASON:
all year round

PROPAGATION:
suckers, crown, ratoon (a new shoot that grows from the root after the old growth has been cut back)

CULINARY USES:
eaten fresh, as juice, puddings, ice cream

OTHER USES:
medicinal, leaves used for clothing

It was claimed, long ago, that 'a young fruit taken with beer on an empty stomach causes what looks like cholera'.

Ananas comosus

PINEAPPLE

(Thai name: *sup-pa-rot*)

Origin:
Brazil and Paraguay

Location:
Tropical lowlands below 800 m

Varieties:
Various—for desserts, canning and ornamental

Originating from South America, the pineapple's cultivation (yes, we hear you, Hawaii!) has become identified with Southeast Asia. Its Malay name, *nanas,* is taken from a Brazilian one (*ananá*), but the name 'pineapple' is an European term, because Christopher Columbus called it 'pines of the Indies' as he and the Spaniards found it to resemble a huge pine cone.

When Columbus brought the pineapple back to Europe, it became known as 'the noblest of all fruits in India' and was served as a status symbol on the tables of the rich and the famous. It was the Spaniards and Portuguese who brought it to Southeast Asia, where it became a staple fruit. The West Indians place a pineapple or its top at the entrance of their homes as a sign of welcome, a custom adopted by the Spaniards.

Pineapples do not travel well and only became exportable with the rise of the pineapple-canning industry. This industry was reputedly started by a French sailor who, jumping ship at Singapore in the 1870s, made a living selling his home-canned pineapples to ships calling at the port.

Most often eaten fresh, the fruit is at times laced with salt to bring out its sweetness and neutralize its acidity. It is also used as a vegetable in Chinese and Thai cuisine and is a frequent ingredient in the multifarious curries of the region. Its role in desserts and cakes is well established. An enzyme in the fruit, which becomes inactive above 104°F (40°C), causes egg whites to split and milk products to turn bitter.

As a home remedy, traditionally it was used as a purgative, powerful enough to cause abortions, and was also taken to cure gonorrhoea. It is recommended for low blood pressure, general debility and indigestion with vomiting.

Its juice was used to rid the blade of a new *keris* (Malay dagger) of its impurities. The fibres from the pineapple's leaves once made fishing lines and sewing thread, and in Manila are still being used to produce *pinya* cloth for the *barong-tagalog* shirt, the national dress of Filipino men. In Thailand it has inspired skilful woodcarvers in their tableware designs.

SINGAPORE SLING

Ingredients:

- 30ml/1oz gin
- 15ml/1/2oz cherry brandy
- 120ml/4oz pineapple juice
- 15ml/1/2oz lime juice
- 7.5ml/1/2oz Cointreau
- 7.5ml/1/2tbsp Dom Benedictine
- 10ml/2/3tbsp Grenadine
- a dash of Angostura Bitters
- pineapple wedge and cherry for garnish

Method: Put all ingredients except the garnish in a cocktail shaker. Shake and serve over crushed ice in a tall glass. Garnish with pineapple wedge and cherry.

The famed Singapore Sling was created at Raffles Hotel at the turn-of-the-century by Hainanese-Chinese bartender Mr. Ngiam Tong Boon. It was originally meant as a lady's drink, hence the attractive pink colour. Visitors to the Raffles Hotel Museum may view the safe in which Mr. Ngiam locked away his precious recipe books, as well as the Singapore Sling recipe hastily jotted down on a bar-chit in 1936 by a visitor who got it from a waiter.

Courtesy of *Raffles Hotel, Singapore*

The numerous reddish-purple flowers of the pineapple open early in the morning and fade away by the evening. The lower flowers of the inflorescence open first, followed by the upper ones—almost in the sequence of their growth. The entire process takes from 20 to 25 days.

DIMENSIONS:

tree:
height: up to 10 m

fruit:
length: 12–24 cm
weight: 400–800 gm

SEASON:
almost all the year round

PROPAGATION:
seeds, budding, grafting

CULINARY USES:
eaten fresh as fruit; made into cakes and beverages; for flavouring

OTHER USES:
medicinal

The soursop's Indonesian name, sirsak, is derived from the Dutch zuur zak meaning 'sour sack'. The English word 'sop' perhaps has been given to signify something that soaks up liquid.

In Indonesia, dodol sirsak, a sweetmeat, is made by boiling soursop pulp in water and adding sugar until the mixture hardens. In the Philippines, a young soursop, where the seeds are still soft, is used as a vegetable. The delicate flavour and aroma of the mature, yet firm, fruit make it an ideal ingredient for making candies.

Annona muricata

SOURSOP

Origin:
Tropical America

Distribution:
Tropical lowlands up to 500 m

Varieties:
About nine, differing in shape, texture and flavour

If its various Malay/Indonesian names are anything to go by, the soursop travelled around the world both ways from its tropical American homeland to reach new tropical destinations. Common Malay names for the fruit are *durian belanda* and *durian mekah* (Dutch and Meccan durian), suggesting their journey from the West, but there is also the name *nangka menila* (Manila jackfruit), indicating its arrival from the East. Its form does suggest a similarity to the durian, and its flesh bears some resemblance to the pulpy flesh of the jackfruit. But the soursop is related to neither.

Soursop belongs to the family Annonaceae which has several delicious fruit, four of which were swiftly introduced to other parts of the tropics by the Spaniards and Portuguese soon after the fruit were discovered. Amongst these, which include the custard apple and sugar apple, the soursop is the best known and has the most delectable flavour.

The soursop is a large fruit of a small, fast-growing tree. The fruit is picked from the tree before it is fully ripe as it will be badly bruised if allowed to ripen and fall. The fruit is mature and is ready for eating when it feels slightly soft and is light green externally. However, the raw fruit can be eaten as a vegetable. The skin is thin and is covered with conical nibs. The white, pulpy flesh, which contains juice, is peppered with small, shiny, black inedible seeds, and has a pleasant, sweet-acidic taste. As it is rather fibrous, its squeezed juice makes a better choice, and has, in fact, become more popular than the fresh fruit as such. The fruit has a high sugar content, about 68 per cent of the total solids, and is a good source of vitamins B and C. The juice makes an excellent sorbet and flavouring for ice creams. In the West Indies, the fruit is fermented to make an apple cider-like drink.

SOURSOP SORBET

Ingredients:
2 ripe soursop/2 generous cups
500gm/2-1/3cups sugar
500ml/2cups water
2gm/1tsp powdered nutmeg
2gm/1tsp powdered cloves

Method: Cut soursop in half, scoop out the flesh and remove seeds. Purée the flesh. Bring water to a boil, add sugar and stir until it has dissolved. Remove from heat and add spices. Stir and strain. Pour syrup into puréed soursop. Chill before serving. Serves one.

The leaves of the soursop are used in traditional medicine to make poultices for sores and wounds, and infusions of the juice, in various combinations, are used to treat skin diseases, cough and rheumatism. The seeds, which have emetic properties, can be used in the treatment of vomiting.

The flowers are solitary and large and covered by two layers of thick fleshy petals which envelop the button-like inner part.

DIMENSIONS:

tree:
height: 4.5–10 m

fruit:
diameter: 8–16 cm
weight: 200 gm–1 kg

SEASON:
almost all the year round

PROPAGATION:
seeds, also budding, grafting

CULINARY USES:
eaten fresh or made into juice and ice cream

OTHER USES:
medicinal, tanning and dyeing

One of the simplest and tastiest ways of enjoying the fruit is by chilling it, breaking it open into two halves, and scooping the pulp into your mouth with a spoon. The seeds naturally will have to be spat out!

In the West Indies, its leaves are used for tanning and for making blue or black dyes.

A decoction of the leaves is a traditional vermifuge, and the juice is claimed to be a useful means of getting rid of lice, while the seeds, leaves and young fruit are insecticidal.

Annona reticulata

CUSTARD APPLE

Origin:
West Indies

Distribution:
Throughout the tropics between 200 and 700 m

Varieties:
Several, depending upon the number of seeds

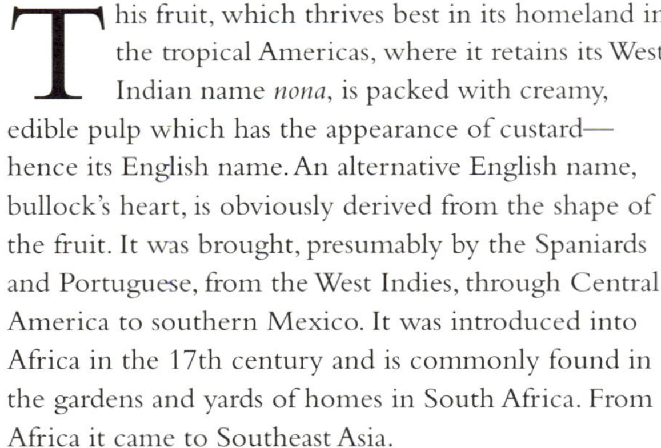

This fruit, which thrives best in its homeland in the tropical Americas, where it retains its West Indian name *nona*, is packed with creamy, edible pulp which has the appearance of custard—hence its English name. An alternative English name, bullock's heart, is obviously derived from the shape of the fruit. It was brought, presumably by the Spaniards and Portuguese, from the West Indies, through Central America to southern Mexico. It was introduced into Africa in the 17th century and is commonly found in the gardens and yards of homes in South Africa. From Africa it came to Southeast Asia.

The Spanish-speaking people call it *anon* or *rinon* and in India it is called *sitaphal* or *ramphal*. Belonging to a family of trees (Annonaceae) whose fruits are very delicious, nevertheless the custard apple is valued more as a rootstock for other trees of the genus rather than as a fruit in its own right. Not a particularly attractive tree, it has ill-smelling leaves with prominent veins. The flowers are fragrant and slender and never open fully.

The lop-sided or heart-shaped fruit with a deep depression at the base has a tough skin with characteristic round protuberances on the surface. Beneath this lies a creamy, custard-like flesh. In this are juicy, translucent segments, each of which contains a shiny, black seed. There are an average of between 50 and 75 seeds in each fruit.

To tell if the fruit is ripe, touch the skin, which ought to be slightly soft to the touch. Discolouration of the light green skin, making it appear black in parts, does not mean that the fruit is bad. As the custard apple ripens very quickly, and the skin ruptures easily, it does not lend itself well to transportation.

The tree possesses a variety of applications in traditional medicine. For boils, abscesses and ulcers, a paste of the de-seeded flesh may be applied. The unripe fruit, dried in the sun and pulverized, is reputedly an effective remedy for diarrhoea and dysentery. Pieces of the root bark, applied to the gums, are found effective for toothache. The plant is also used in the treatment of epilepsy and convulsions. The fruit is a rich source of fibre and vitamin A, yet at the same time is high in calories.

CUSTARD APPLE AND TROPICAL FRUIT *PAKORA* WITH TANDOORI CHICKEN

Pakora (dumplings)

Ingredients:

60gm/2oz custard apple, grated
20gm/2tbsp rambutan flesh
15gm/1tbsp pomegranate seeds
20gm/2tbsp banana, diced
15gm/1tbsp banana flower, julienne

Pakora batter

(mix in water to make coating consistency)

Ingredients:

150gm/1-1/2 cup *besan* (chickpea/gram flour)
150gm/1-1/2 cup plain flour
1/2 tsp baking powder
salt and pepper to taste
vegetable oil to fry

Tandoori chicken

Ingredients:

120gm/4oz chicken breast (with bone)
30gm/2tbsp tandoori powder, made into paste with a little 1/4 cup yogurt

Method: Marinate chicken in yogurt paste for 6 hours. Bake at 220°C for 20 minutes. Mix *pakora* ingredients, and make small balls. Dip in batter and deep fry till golden brown. Drain off excess oil. Place *pakora* and chicken on plate. Garnish with yogurt drizzle.

Serves 2

Courtesy of *Marriott Surfers Paradise Resort, Australia*

The flesh of the custard apple is reminiscent of custard— and is said to taste like a blend of pineapple, papaya and mango—and vanilla custard!

DIMENSIONS:

tree:
height: 3–6 m

fruit:
diameter: 6–10 cm
weight: 100–150 gm

SEASON:
almost all year round

PROPAGATION:
seeds; budding; grafting

CULINARY USES:
eaten raw as fruit

OTHER USES:
medicinal

The fruit of this family contain no sodium. They are high in carbohydrates and rich in calcium, vitamin C and phosphorus. The sugar content is about 50-50 glucose and sucrose.

In Mexico, the leaves are used as a lice repellent for poultry. The leaves are rubbed on the floor and placed in the hens' nests.

The best way of eating the delicious fruit of this family is to split open the fruit, scoop a spoonful of pulp into the mouth, enjoy the fleshy segments while separating the hard seeds in the mouth, and spitting them out.

Annona squamosa

SUGAR APPLE

Origin:
West Indies

Distribution:
Tropical lowlands up to 300 m

Varieties:
About ten, varying in size, shape, though similar in flavour

This highly rated member of the *Annona* genus, which originally grew in the West Indies, was spread by the Spaniards and the Portuguese to other parts of the tropical world. The latter also introduced it to southern India before 1590.

The fruit has a rough, knobbly, greyish-green exterior in which is encased a creamy, white pulp which thinly envelops a host of shiny, dark brown seeds. Besides its derived American name, the apple-sized and heart-shaped fruit is given a Malay name *serikaya* (which literally translates as 'rich in grace'), due to the delicacy of its taste.

The fruit is generally eaten fresh. The pulp serves as the basis of a delicious ice cream. With a sugar content of 10 per cent, the taste is sweet.

The sugar apple has a number of applications in traditional medicine, some of them seemingly contradictory. Its pulpy leaves serve both as a purgative and also to cure diarrhoea. They can also be applied to abscesses and open wounds and used to cure skin itches. The seeds, immersed in coconut oil, form a traditional treatment for head and body lice. The roots of the sugar apple tree also work as a purgative and are powerful enough to induce abortions. In some parts of India, crushed leaves are sniffed to overcome fainting spells and hysteria, while the mashed, ripe fruit, mixed with salt, is applied on tumours. Across tropical America, a decoction of the leaves is used as a digestive aid, to treat colds and to relieve rheumatic pains.
The green fruit and seeds have both vermicidal and insecticidal properties.

The most widely grown of all the Annona species, the sugar apple has various regional names. In Central and South America it is called anon, anon de azucar, anona blanca, anona de castilla, and anona de Guatemala (but not in Guatemala, where it is known as chirimoya!). It is sweetsop in Jamaica and the Bahamas, sharifa, or sitaphal in India, and further east, it is manonah or a grand-sounding pomme cannelle du Cap in Thailand, qu a na in Vietnam, mang cau ta in Cambodia, mah khbieb in Laos and fan-li-chi in China.

As the flower of the fruit of the genus Annona contain several ovaries, the custard apple, sugar apple and soursop are produced by the fusion of numerous florets under a common rind. In this aggregate fruit the separate parts are not so tightly packed, and the fruit tends to come apart quite easily when it is ripe.

DIMENSIONS:
tree:
height: up to 10.6 m
fruit:
diameter: 8–10 mm

SEASON:
February and March

PROPAGATION:
seeds, marcotting

CULINARY USES:
eaten fresh; taken as juice; used in preparation of sauce for fish dishes

OTHER USES:
medicinal (bark)

Antidesma bunius

Bignay

Origin:
India

Distribution:
South Asia, insular Southeast Asia to northern Australia

Varieties:
One or two

Although a native of India, bignay is found across the subcontinent, from the foothills of the Himalayas in the north, down to Kanya Kumari (Cape Comorin) in the south, and further south to the island of Sri Lanka. This fruit is more popular in its second home in Indonesia and Malaysia. It is particularly popular in Java and Sulawesi where it is grown in nearly every village. Indeed, its Malay name *buni* or *berunai* may well have been the source of the name of the State of Brunei, and by extension that of the island of Borneo as well.

The tree is an evergreen, with wide, dark-green glossy, leathery leaves, and the bark contains a toxic alkaloid. The reddish flowers are tiny and have an obnoxious smell. Male and female flowers are produced on separate trees. The tree is valued for its berries, which are generally eaten raw. The round fruit is borne in grape-like clusters and it is their different stages of ripening simultaneously that gives the bignay tree a highly attractive appearance and which has made it popular as a decorative garden tree in Indonesia. It is normal to find a single pendant cluster bearing a range of white, yellow, pale green, red and black berries. While the thin yet tough skin is coloured and yields a red juice, the pulp within is white and contains a colourless acidic liquid. Each fruit has a single seed.

The fruit is more sour than sweet, and is used for making jam. In Indonesia and in the Philippines, the fruit is cooked with fish dishes and the leaves are stewed with rice and other vegetables to give flavour, or are sometimes even eaten raw.

In Asia, the leaves of the bignay are used in the treatment of snakebite. The bark contains a strong fibre which is used for making ropes. The reddish, hard wood has been experimented with to make cardboard.

The bignay tree is prone to infestation. While in Southeast Asia the trees are attacked by termites, in Florida the leaves may be attacked by scale insects and mealy bugs.

The bignay is known as currant tree, salamander tree and wild cherry in English. In the Philippines it is bignai and buni and in Malaysia, berunai. It is wooni in Indonesia, choi moi in Vietnam; and ma mao luang in Thailand. The aborigines in Queensland call it chunka.

In the United States, the juice, which makes an excellent syrup, has been successfully fermented to make wine and brandy.

To improve the flavour of bignay juice: keep the juice in a glass or plastic container and refrigerate for a day or two. An astringent sediment will settle at the bottom. Pour the juice carefully into another vessel and discard the sediment.

Artocarpus altilis

BREADFRUIT

(Thai name: *sa-ke*)

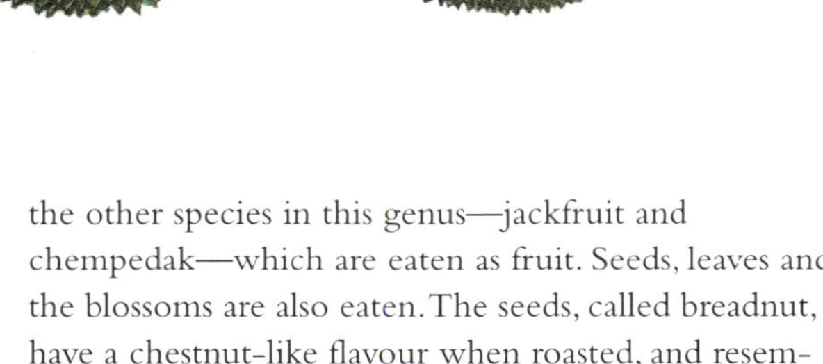

Origin:
South Pacific, Polynesia

Location:
In the tropics, up to 1000 m

Varieties:
Seeded and seedless

DIMENSIONS:
tree:
height: 20 m

fruit: seed
diameter: 20–25 cm
weight: 0.5–3 kg
fruit: seedless
diameter: 5-20 cm
weight: 0.5–1 kg

SEASON:
almost all year round

PRODUCTIVITY:
up to 25–30 years

PROPAGATION:
seeds; root cuttings

CULINARY USES:
as a vegetable; in desserts

OTHER USES:
medicinal purposes

Its tall trunk is swathed in 'very large, dark green leaves', against which 'the paler green of the fruit stand out like candles',
—I. H. Burkill, A Dictionary of the Economic Products of the Malay Peninsula.

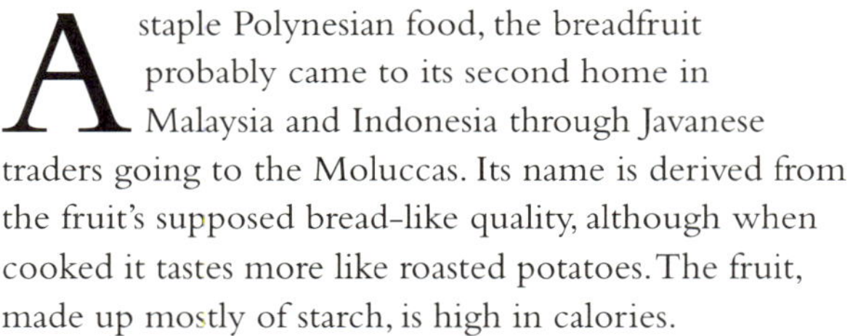

A staple Polynesian food, the breadfruit probably came to its second home in Malaysia and Indonesia through Javanese traders going to the Moluccas. Its name is derived from the fruit's supposed bread-like quality, although when cooked it tastes more like roasted potatoes. The fruit, made up mostly of starch, is high in calories.

The fruit's bread-like properties made sensational news in the 18th century, persuading British sugar planters in the Caribbean of its potential as a food for their workers. The breadfruit was the cause of the mutiny against Captain Bligh of the *HMS Bounty* in 1787 when he sailed from Tahiti with his cargo of the fruit's seedlings. A second expedition fared better, and the breadfruit was transported to the West Indies, where it has since thrived mightily.

A 10-year-old tree will produce 300 to 700 breadfruits each year, weighing 2 to 3 kilograms each. Thus the yield potential is approximately 600 to 2000 kilograms per tree per year.

Breadfruit (which must be cooked before it is eaten) is used primarily as a vegetable, unlike the other species in this genus—jackfruit and chempedak—which are eaten as fruit. Seeds, leaves and the blossoms are also eaten. The seeds, called breadnut, have a chestnut-like flavour when roasted, and resemble *marrons glacés* if boiled in sugar.

Most Southeast Asians use breadfruit to flavour local curries. Its flesh, when dried, is ground into flour to make biscuits. The fruit is highly perishable and is traditionally stored by submerging it in water.

To Polynesians, the threat of cyclones, droughts, and the complete destruction of their crops by enemies were a constant danger to their existence. These pressures led to the development of food preservation techniques. Breadfruit and bananas were peeled and wrapped in airtight packets using heliconia and banana leaves. They were then buried, which allowed them to ferment, but not rot. When required, the food was then baked with coconut cream and eaten.

The latex has cementing properties and is applied to the caulking of boats. Mixed with mud, it doubles as a paint for the boats. There are also some medicinal applications of the fruit.

BINGKANG SUKUN (breadfruit cake)

Ingredients:
500gm/2cups ripe breadfruit
3 eggs
250gm/2cups flour
50gm/1/4cup brown sugar, lightly packed
750ml/3cups coconut milk
2gm/1/4tsp salt

Method: Beat eggs in a bowl. Add sugar and mix till dissolved. Add flour, mashed breadfruit and coconut milk alternately and stir slowly. Add salt and mix. Pour in a greased pan. Bake in an oven at moderate heat for an hour until brown and firm. Cool and slice.

Captain James Cook, on one of his voyages to Polynesia, described cooked breadfruit as being 'hardly distinguishable from an excellent batter pudding'.
—Jacqueline M. Piper, Fruits of South-East Asia

DIMENSIONS:

tree:
height: 10–20 m length

fruit:
diameter: 25–50 cm
length: 30–100 cm
weight: 5–40 kg
(average 16 kg)

SEASON:
all the year round

PROPAGATION:
seeds, budding

CULINARY USES:
eaten fresh; cooked as vegetable; prepared as a delicacy; seeds edible after cooking

OTHER USES:
medicinal (juice and leaves); as a dye, the wood is used as timber

The jackfruit was first known to the Western world from the writings of Pliny the Elder, a naturalist who lived about AD 100.

'Fall Nangka if you must, but not on the branches of the Pauh. Close your sleepy eyes and sleep, and do not ponder on the memories of someone far away.'
—Malay pantun

Artocarpus heterophyllus

JACKFRUIT

(Thai name: *kha-noon*)

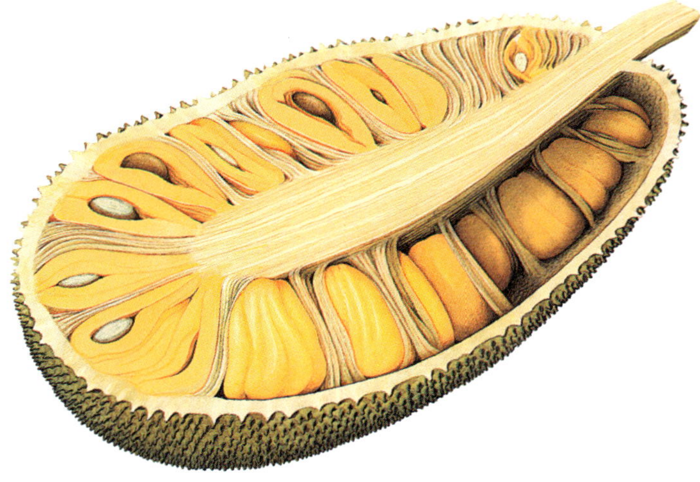

Origin:
India

Distribution:
South and Southeast Asia, east Africa, parts of tropical America

Varieties:
Two main varieties based on flesh of fruit: firm and soft

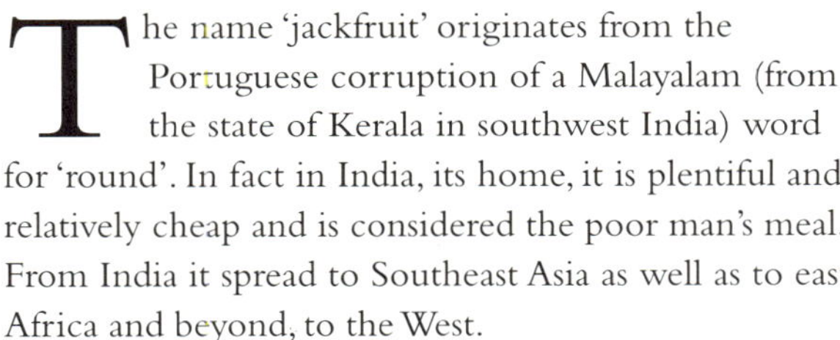

The name 'jackfruit' originates from the Portuguese corruption of a Malayalam (from the state of Kerala in southwest India) word for 'round'. In fact in India, its home, it is plentiful and relatively cheap and is considered the poor man's meal. From India it spread to Southeast Asia as well as to east Africa and beyond, to the West.

The jackfruit has the distinction of being the largest fruit on earth and is borne on the main branches and trunk of the tree. It can grow to an enormous 40 kilograms, one fruit being sufficient to feed an entire family. The thick, pale to deep green rind is dotted with hexagonal spines and is fed to livestock. Inside the rind is a layer of thick white pith. Within the fruit is a fibrous material called 'rags'. Embedded in the rags is the yellow flesh, in the form of capsules. This in turn envelops the seeds, which are edible and highly nutritious. The flesh is almost rubbery in consistency and has a distinct odour which may be offensive to the uninitiated nostril.

The fruit is highly nutritious, with a carbohydrate content of almost 40 per cent, 6 per cent protein and 0.4 per cent fat. When ripe the jackfruit is eaten fresh, while unripe fruit serves as a vegetable in many a local dish. The fruit may also end up in soups, ice creams (as a flavour), and fruit salad. Its seeds, if boiled and then roasted, make a tasty offering redolent of chestnuts. The fruit is also pickled. As the fruit contains a sticky latex, it is advisable to rub cooking oil on your hands, the chopping board and knife before cutting it.

Jackfruit timber is stout and of good quality, and is used in constructing houses, and because of its deep yellow colour it was the preferred choice for royal palaces in Bali and Makassar (Sulawesi) and for temples in Vietnam. Commonly used for making furniture as well, in the Philippines it is also used for crafting musical instruments. When boiled, the wood produces a deep orange-yellow dye, which in earlier times was much favoured by Buddhist monks for dyeing their saffron robes.

ANDAMAN TUNA WITH *MAE JOM** JACKFRUIT SALSA

Jackfruit salsa
Ingredients:
200gm/6oz flesh of jackfruit
60gm/2oz freshly sliced Thai shallots
45ml/3tbsp rice vinegar
dash of Thai fish sauce
freshly-ground pepper and salt to taste

Rice and fish
150gm/2/3 cup dry weight Thai jasmine fragrant rice steamed with lemon grass and galangal (blue ginger/*lengkuas*)
45ml/3tbsp vegetable oil
300gm/10oz fresh pencil asparagus
15gm/5 garlic cloves, chopped
15gm/2tbsp chopped ginger
4 pcs centre cut tuna (each weighing 160gm/5oz)

Garnish
12gm/3tbsp chopped purple basil
24gm/2tbsp dry rice powder
2 gm/1 medium size red chilli, de-seeded, thinly sliced and deep fried

Method: Marinate jackfruit and all other salsa ingredients for 2 hours. Pan sear tuna for about a minute on each side. Set aside. Slice each piece tuna into half at an angle and pour marinade. Stir fry asparagus with ginger and garlic. Serve tuna with rice and asparagus. Garnish with chilli, basil and rice powder. Serves 4.

* *named in honour of the chef's mother-in-law*

Courtesy of *JW Marriott Hotel, Hong Kong*

DIMENSIONS:
tree:
height: up to 18 m
fruit:
length: up to 35 cm
width: 15 cm
weight: up to 25 kg

SEASON:
all the year round

PROPAGATION:
seeds

CULINARY USES:
flesh eaten raw; seeds cooked; as a pickle

OTHER USES:
as a timber; in dyeing

Artocarpus integer

CHEMPEDAK

Origin:
Indonesia, Malaysia, Thailand and Myanmar

Distribution:
Throughout Southeast Asia

Varieties:
There are various cultivated and wild varieties

'If the chempedak is outside
the fence,
Take a stick to make it fall,
I am a boy who has just
started to learn,
If I am wrong, please show
me how.'
— Malay proverb

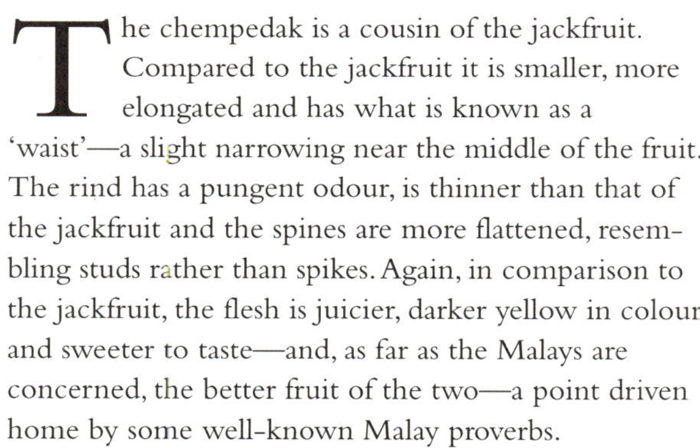

The chempedak is a cousin of the jackfruit. Compared to the jackfruit it is smaller, more elongated and has what is known as a 'waist'—a slight narrowing near the middle of the fruit. The rind has a pungent odour, is thinner than that of the jackfruit and the spines are more flattened, resembling studs rather than spikes. Again, in comparison to the jackfruit, the flesh is juicier, darker yellow in colour and sweeter to taste—and, as far as the Malays are concerned, the better fruit of the two—a point driven home by some well-known Malay proverbs.

The chempedak was taken by the Arabs to the east coast of Africa and finally to tropical Africa.

The cultivated species, of which there are several, were said to have evolved from the wild variety called *bankong* which flourishes in the jungles. Yet another theory, based on recent studies in Sarawak, shows that there are no consistent differences between the wild and cultivated varieties. This implies that the cultivated chempedak is not derived from the wild *bankong*. The latter is perhaps an isolated form. The wild tree grows to a bigger size and is more prolific in its seeds.

The yellow, custard-like flesh which envelopes the seeds is eaten fresh. But the peoples of the forest—especially the aborigines of the Malay Peninsula—regard the seeds, which they 'pluck, split and boil', as being far more nutritious and filling. There are between 100 and 500 seeds in each fruit, and the flesh surrounding the seeds has the appearance of grapes. The seeds are also eaten roasted or boiled in salty water, while young leaves are cooked as a vegetable.

Of the three fruits from the *Artocarpus* genus—jackfruit, chempedak and breadfruit—the chempedak tree bears the most fruit which, though smaller in size, is yet the most expensive among the three.

The medium-sized evergreen tree, like that of the jackfruit, has a smooth grey bark when young, which becomes rough, thick, and furrowed with age. The strong, durable timber is used for making furniture and in the construction of both houses and boats. The yellowish sap from the heartwood is used in Cambodia, Laos, and the Mekong Delta in south Vietnam as a dye for the saffron robes of Buddhist monks. The bark can be used to make rope.

FRIED CHEMPEDAK

Ingredients:
250gm/2cup flour
salt to taste
1 egg yolk and 12gm/1tbs castor sugar (beaten together)
250ml/1cup warm milk
20–30 chempedak segments
1 egg white (beaten stiffly)
cooking oil for deep frying

Method: Sift flour and salt into a mixing bowl. Make a well in the centre and pour in the egg yolk and sugar mix. Add warm milk slowly. Beat until the batter is smooth. Just before use add the stiffly beaten egg white. Heat oil for deep frying. Roll the chempedak in dry flour seasoned with a little salt before dipping in the batter. Fry 5-6 at a time until golden brown (heat oil before putting in each batch to fry). Remove and drain on grease-absorbent paper. Serve hot.

A very popular Malaysian snack is made from the flesh of the chempedak. The seed is removed from the segment and the flesh is naturally a round 'ball'. Dip into a batter of rice flour, sugar, milk and water and deep fry till golden brown.

DIMENSIONS:
tree: height: up to 6 m
fruit: length: 5 cm diameter: 1–2 cm
SEASON: almost all year round
PROPAGATION: seeds
CULINARY USES: used as seasoning for curries and for pickles, chutneys and preserves
OTHER USES: traditional medicine (juice and leaves)

Averrhoa bilimbi

BILIMBI

(Thai name: *ta-ling-pling*)

Origin:

Malaysia, Thailand and Indonesia

Distribution:

Tropics up to a height of 500 m

The Malays call the extremely sour bilimbi fruit *belimbing asam* (*asam*—sour) to distinguish it from the starfruit or *belimbing manis* (*manis*—sweet) to which it is closely allied. The British, during the colonial times, bestowed on this fruit its only English names—cucumber tree and tree sorrel. *Bilimbi* is the common name widely used in India and in the region. In Indonesia it is called *belimbing besu*; in Thailand it is *taling pling* and in the Philippines, *kamais*. In other parts of the world where it grows, it has as many names. In Haiti it is *blimblin*; in Cuba, *grosella china*; in El Salvador and Nicaragua, *mimbro* or *tiriguro*; *vinagrillo* in Venezula; *birambi* in Surinam and Guyana; and in Argentina *pepino de Indias*. The French call it *carambolier bilimbi* or *cornichon des Indes*.

The tree is quite attractive, with its short trunk dividing into many upright branches which have clusters of leaves, mainly at the tips. The flowers are small, deep red and have a strong, sweet scent.

The narrow, oblong fruit has five shallow ridges running along its length, and a smooth, thin skin. The fruit, which is widely available, is useful in the making of seasonings for curries and for pickling, and is substituted for mango in chutney.

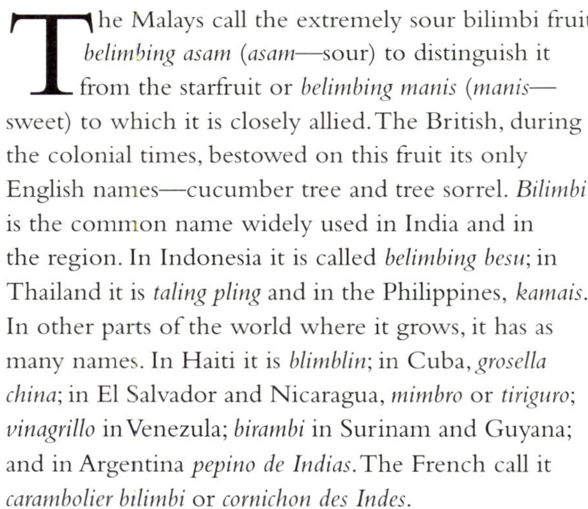

The flowers of the bilimbi tree can be preserved with sugar and then eaten.

The bilimbi is regarded as too acidic for eating raw, but in some countries, such as Costa Rica, the green, uncooked fruit is prepared as a relish and served with rice and beans. In countries in the Far East, the ripe fruit is added to curries. The juice of the fruit is popular for making cooling and refreshing drinks similar to lemonade.

The high acid content of the juice makes it a suitable agent for removing stains from the skin and from textiles. In olden days it was used for cleaning the blade of a *keris,* the short, wavy dagger of the Malays.

Traditional medicinal uses of the bilimbi are quite remarkable. One particular Javanese preparation which includes pepper is used to induce perspiration. The Javanese also use concoctions of its leaves as a remedy for mumps, rheumatism and pimples. Malays use its pickle in a paste to alleviate fever and itches, while the juice is effective as eye drops (regarded as a magic curative). The leaves, fresh or fermented, are often consumed as a cure for syphilis. The bilimbi is given to children as a protection against coughs, while in parts of the Philippines the juice is made into a syrup to counter fevers.

To reduce acidity, prick the bilimbi and soak overnight in water, or in salt and water for a shorter time.

The half-ripe bilimbi fruit is salted, dried in the sun and pickled in brine. It can then be preserved for up to three months.

SAMBAL TUMIS BELIMBI (chilli bilimbi relish)

Ingredients:
20gm/20 whole dried chillies
2gm/1/2tsp *belacan* (shrimp paste)
8gm/3 medium cloves garlic
50ml/1/5cup tamarind juice
3gm/1cm piece fresh turmeric
90ml/2tbsp oil
3gm/1/2tsp salt
250gm/2 medium onions (1 for frying)
5 bilimbi, sliced
24gm/2tbsp sugar
2cm ginger

Method: Soak dried chillies in water for one hour. Drain and wash. Blend chillies with all ingredients except one onion and bilimbi. Heat oil in saucepan. Fry one chopped onion till soft. Pour in blended ingredients. Cook for about 20 minutes over a slow fire. Add salt, 2 tbsp water, tamarind juice and sugar. Add bilimbi and cook for 10 minutes. Serve with rice or as a dipping sauce.

DIMENSIONS:

tree:
height: 5–12 m

fruit:
length: 10–20 cm
diameter: 6–10 cm
weight: 150–500 gm

SEASON:
almost all year round

PRODUCTIVITY:
20–39 years

PROPAGATION:
seeds, grafting, marcotting

CULINARY USES:
eaten as fresh fruit and in salads; a syrup; a pickle

OTHER USES:
medicinal; stain remover

Averrhoa carambola

STAR FRUIT/CARAMBOLA

(Thai name: *ma-fuang*)

Origin:
Southeast Asia

Distribution:
Tropics and frost-free subtropics up to 500 m

Varieties:
Several, ranging from sweet to sour

Tiny lilac flowers are produced in panicles on the twigs as well as the tree trunk. The individual flower stalks and buds are deep pink or red.

Averrhoa—the scientific name for this genus of fruit—is named for Averroës (Ibn Rushd), the 12th-century Spanish Islamic astronomer, doctor and philosopher. The species, and common, name, *carambola*, is a Portuguese word derived from Malayalam, a south Indian language. Star fruit, its other common name, describes the shape of a cross-section slice of the fruit.

The tree was introduced to the Malay Peninsula from other parts of Southeast Asia by early Arab and Indian traders. It is now grown widely throughout the region, and in countries, such as Australia. In Malaysia, it has been found to grow well on tin-tailings, the sandy soil of former tin mining areas (areas not suitable for many other crops). Although this is a labour-intensive crop as the individual fruit must be wrapped to prevent insect attack, a flourishing export trade has developed.

Groups of three or four fruit are borne on the trunk and branches of the tree. Green when raw, the fruit vary from pale yellow to deep amber when ripe. The five-angled, unique-shaped fruit has soft flesh encased in a thin waxy, translucent skin (which is eaten together with the flesh). The fruit, which is mostly consumed fresh or as juice, is rich in vitamins A and C and iron, and has a high fibre content. The taste varies from acid—a favourite antidote to which is to eat it with sugar and dark soya sauce—to sweet. One way of distinguishing the sour variety from the sweeter ones is that the former has narrower ribs, while the latter have thicker, fleshy ones.

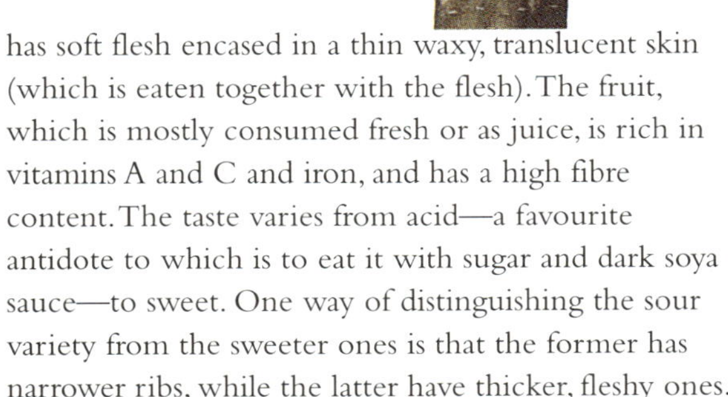

A versatile remedy, its leaves and roots, prepared separately or in combination in various ways, have cured headaches, ringworm, and chickenpox. Carambola is known to cure hangovers, and prickly heat. It has also been used to treat sore eyes. The star fruit is given to nursing mothers as it is commonly believed to stimulate the flow of milk.

STAR FRUIT DRINK

Ingredients:
5 ripe star fruit
60ml/juice from 6 limes
500ml/2 cups water
36gm/3tbsp granulated sugar
125gm/1/2 cup lychee syrup
1-2 drops yellow colouring

Method: Cut edges from all angles of the fruit. Halve and remove seeds. Cut into thin slices. Cover with lime juice. Make syrup by boiling sugar and water, stirring constantly until sugar dissolves. Strain and cool. Put fruit into a glass jug. Pour in sugar syrup and lychee syrup. Mix in yellow colouring to obtain a pale yellow colour. Chill in refrigerator and serve with crushed ice. Serves 4.

Unripe star fruit is preserved in many parts of Southeast Asia and is used as a traditional remedy. Take sliced fruit and place in sun till half dry. Cover in vinegar (pickled); salt (salted) or sugar (sweet) and use as needed.

For sunstroke, a piece of the sweet version is recommended; for nausea and indigestion eat half a piece of the pickled fruit and repeat after three hours. For a hangover, take one piece of the pickled fruit, steam in water and serve.

DIMENSIONS:
tree: height: 2–25 m
fruit: diameter (individual fruit): 10–20 cm weight (per bunch): 500 gm–1 kg
SEASON: all the year round
PROPAGATION: seeds
CULINARY USES: as a food; a drink; source of sugar (jaggery)
OTHER USES: numerous, in particular the leaf

Borassus flabellifer

SEA APPLE

Origin:

South Asia and Southeast Asia

Distribution:

Less humid tropical areas of Africa, Arabia, South and Southeast Asia up to 500 m

Varieties:

Numerous 'strains' or types depending upon fruit shape or size

Quite significantly, the palm's leaves were used as writing material until the advent of paper. In fact the early documents of South and Southeast Asia were inscribed on the palmyra or lontar leaf. Incidentally, lontar, the Malay word for the tree and its fruit, comes from the Sanskrit term for the palm 'tala' and 'ron' which translates as 'leaf'— the word lontar being a variant of it.

The sea apple, which is the fruit of the palmyra or sugar palm, is popularly known as *lontar* in Malaysia and Indonesia, vies to be a rival of the coconut. The fact that it is not so is only because its natural area is restricted to the less humid regions of the tropics. Nevertheless, the palm is a formidable tree which is as useful for rural folk in the areas where it flourishes, as is the coconut itself.

The sea apple, as a fruit and a source of food, strongly resembles the coconut in various ways. The large black fruit (nuts), growing in clusters at the base of the leaves, contain a refreshing juice which is enjoyed as a cooling drink and which tastes similar to coconut water. The soft white kernel of the young fruit is eaten fresh or can be cooked. The tree is a copious producer of a sap which can be fermented to produce toddy (a local drink), yeast, vinegar and brown sugar (jaggery). Southeast Asian chefs swear by this variety of sugar as being less cloying than the sugar cane variety. But to tap the juice means to forgo the fruit.

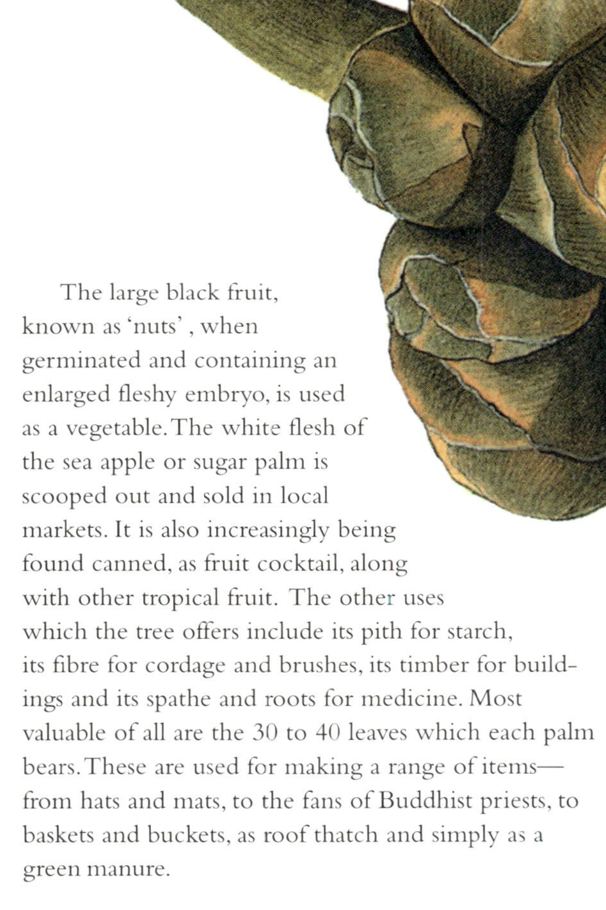

The large black fruit, known as 'nuts' , when germinated and containing an enlarged fleshy embryo, is used as a vegetable. The white flesh of the sea apple or sugar palm is scooped out and sold in local markets. It is also increasingly being found canned, as fruit cocktail, along with other tropical fruit. The other uses which the tree offers include its pith for starch, its fibre for cordage and brushes, its timber for buildings and its spathe and roots for medicine. Most valuable of all are the 30 to 40 leaves which each palm bears. These are used for making a range of items—from hats and mats, to the fans of Buddhist priests, to baskets and buckets, as roof thatch and simply as a green manure.

Sea apples are harvested with the use of long bamboo poles. These are wielded to bring down large bunches of ripe fruit. The young fruit is then kept in a cool place before it is made into a drink. In parts of Southeast Asia this drink is very popular, especially during the Muslim fasting month of Ramadan.

Buckets are made from a single, fan-shaped *lontar* leaf by bringing together the 'fingers' at the outer end of the leaf and securing them to a wooden bar, which is then secured to the other end. These are then used to collect the sap tapped from the palm tree or as a water container.

DIMENSIONS:
tree:
height: up to 27 m
fruit:
diameter: 1–2 cm
weight 50-60 gm

SEASON:
beginning of rainy season

PRODUCTIVITY:
up to 30 years

PROPAGATION:
seeds

CULINARY USES:
as a fruit eaten fresh, preserved in a syrup, made into jam, used in pickling and as an ingredient in certain seasonings

OTHER USES:
traditional medicine (juice and leaves)

In countries of their origin, the best gandaria can demand the same price as a top-of-the-line mango.

If you cut the large, pale, leathery seed/stone in half, you will find two brilliantly coloured—pinkish mauve—seed leaves inside.

Bouea macrophylla

Gandaria

Origin:
Malaysia and Indonesia

Distribution:
Southeast Asia, to a height of up to 500 m

Varieties:
Three or four which are smaller and more acid

Gandaria, a familiar enough fruit in Malaysian and Indonesian villages which has given its name to the State capital of Kedah (Alor Setar), is not so well known outside the region. Yet it belongs to the small group of lesser-known and rare fruit of the region with economic protential. Gandaria is the Javanese name. It is known as *kundang* in Malaysia, but in the Malaysian state of Kedah it is called *setar*. In Thailand it is called *ma praang*.

The gandaria is a decorative, dense, shade tree with low, hanging branches. The tree is distinctive as it has an even, round shape with arched branches and drooping, shiny leathery leaves. The flowers, which grow in stalked bunches, or panicles, are very small and yellowish-green in colour, which soon turn brown.

A mature tree may produce as much as 200 kilograms of fruit in one season. The slightly oblong fruit hanging on the panicles among the leaves are similar to small mangoes. The smooth, soft and thin skin, green at first, then ripens to a deep yellow or orange. There is a large central stone which is leathery in texture, and like the mango's seed, is attached to the flesh by fibres.

The gandaria has an odour—described as being reminiscent of 'the faint smell of turpentine'—which might be mildly repulsive to the uninitiated. It is an acquired flavour, like that of the durian. Yet those who like it find it extremely tasty, very juicy and with a distinct sweet-sour flavour.

The tree's sturdy wood, which in the past was used to make the scabbard of the *keris*, a traditional Malay dagger, was also used in the construction of houses.

While the ripe, sweet-sour fruit is eaten fresh, cooked in a syrup, made into jam, or stewed to make a delicious compote, the immature fruit are also greatly in demand. They are used to make sambal (a shrimp and chilli-based condiment), and in pickles. The young leaves, which are deep violet—or a striking white when just emerging—are eaten with the sambal.

DIMENSIONS:

tree:
height: up to 10 m

fruit:
length: 7–30 cm
diameter: 5–15 cm
weight: 0.4–3 kg

SEASON:
all year round

PRODUCTIVITY:
3 years

PROPAGATION:
seeds; grafting; cutting

CULINARY USES:
as a fruit, vegetable, in salads and jam

OTHER USES:
medicinal; meat tenderizer

Carica papaya

PAPAYA/PAW PAW

(Thai name: *ma-la-kor*)

Origin:
Tropical America (probably Mexico)

Distribution:
In all the warm, humid tropical regions

Varieties:
Numerous, varying in size and flavour

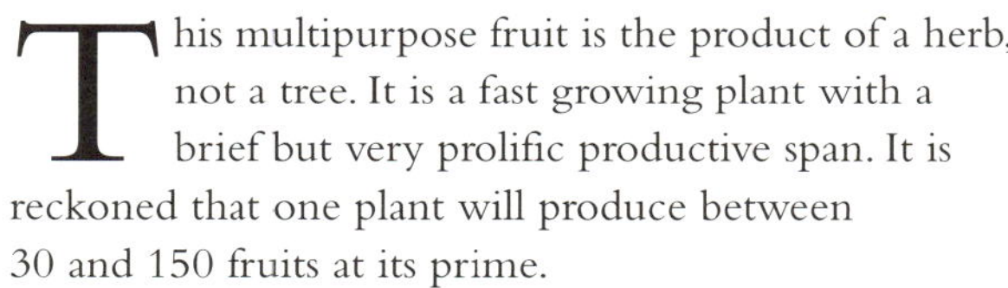

This multipurpose fruit is the product of a herb, not a tree. It is a fast growing plant with a brief but very prolific productive span. It is reckoned that one plant will produce between 30 and 150 fruits at its prime.

The name is of Spanish origin, and it was the Spaniards and the Portuguese who introduced the plant to other tropical regions soon after their American conquests. Among the principal beneficiaries was the Indonesian and Malaysian Archipelago, where it has become a part of the local diet.

The elongated, club-shaped papaya has a mottled green-yellow leathery skin. The thick, sweet flesh can be yellowish- or pinkish-orange. The central part of the fruit is hollow and contains numerous inedible peppercorn-sized black seeds which resemble caviar and have medicinal properties. The fruit consists of 90 per cent water and 10 per cent sugar and other carbohydrates, and has a high content of vitamins A and C and is claimed to have as much calcium as the best orange.

The ripe papaya, which is often served as a breakfast fruit in homes and in hotels, is also frequently offered as a dessert, with a dash of lime juice or some salt and ground red chilli and pepper to sharpen its taste. Unripe papaya serves as a vegetable and appears in a variety of dishes. In the unripe form it is boiled and mashed and fed to babies in India, as the enzyme papain in it is a good digestive aid. The ripe fruit also makes a good jam.

The juice of the papaya is effective for skin blemishes and warts; its leaves, suitably treated, serve as a diuretic and vermifuge, and in certain countries are smoked as a substitute for tobacco or used as a cure for asthma. The juice of an unripe papaya, mixed with vinegar and salt, is used to treat ulcers and other skin infections. A traditional Chinese remedy to increase the flow of milk in lactating mothers was a concoction made by boiling together a half-ripe papaya with pig's trotters. When cooked, the bones were removed, the papaya blended in the soup.

Papain has numerous modern applications which include its use in the preparation of chewing gum, and as an agent for preventing woollens from shrinking.

Linschoten, a 16th-century traveller to Malaysia, documented the presence of Papaios in Malacca.

The enzyme papain, a milky latex in unripe papaya, can split protein, act as a beer clarifier and tenderize meat.

Traditional Chinese food remedies mention papaya as a treatment for tapeworms and roundworms. Take 250 gm sour papaya (skinned and de-seeded raw papaya, soaked in vinegar) and 60 ml of the liquid it was soaked in. Drink for three nights before going to sleep.

PAPAYA SOUFFLÉ WITH CITRUS SALAD

Ingredients:
150ml/3/5cup milk
350gm/1-1/3 cups papaya purée
200gm/1cup sugar
60gm/1/3cup cornflour
50gm/1/3cup flour
225gm/8 egg yolks
300gm/10 egg whites
Citrus Salad (peeled orange slices)

Method: Boil milk with papaya purée and sugar. Dissolve the cornflour and flour with a little cold water and add to the papaya milk mixture and cook, stirring constantly, until it thickens. Whip egg white until white and fluffy. Set aside. Add egg yolks to the cooled, cooked mixture one at a time and stir continuously. Next, carefully fold in egg white and pour the mixture into a buttered and sugared soufflé mould, filling to the top. Bake at 400°C in a water bath for 15 minutes (taking care not to open the oven during this period). Serve with Citrus Salad. Serves 8-10.

Courtesy of *Conrad International Centennial Singapore*

DIMENSIONS:

tree:
height: 4.5–18 m

fruit:
diameter: 7.5–12.5 cm

CULINARY USES:
in drinks but primarily as a dessert fruit in ice cream, pies and other desserts

OTHER USES:
medicinal

'Sapote' which means 'soft fruit' comes from the Mexican word zapotl, or zapote. It is easy to confuse this fruit with a number of others called sapote or sapota that originated in Mexico and Central America.

Casimiroa edulis

CASIMIROA

Origin:
Central and South America

Distribution:
Less humid tropical areas

Varieties:
Many cultivated strains, varying in size and taste

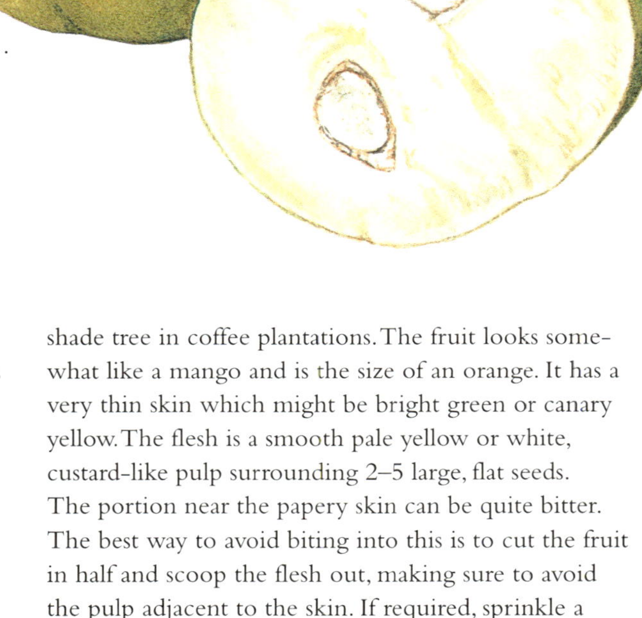

This tropical American fruit, which is also known as white sapote and *zapote blanco*, is originally from the highlands of Mexico and Central America. It has one important attribute that sets its apart from most others, in that its leaves, bark and seed contain a useful glucoside called casimirosine which has the effect of lowering blood pressure. No doubt because of this, in the past it was believed to be a soporific—dangerously so—but modern research has shown that this reputation merely served to make it a useful placebo. As a traditional remedy, extracts of the glucoside were used in large doses as a sedative and to relieve rheumatic pains.

The fruit has a long history, and was well known to the Aztec of Mexico. Being highly perishable after ripening, the fruit is not exported, which is a pity because it has a pleasant taste—'like the best pears'—according to one observer. It has a high sugar content (27 per cent), and is rich in vitamins A and C. At the same time, it is low in calories.

The casimiroa tree, a large evergreen, has a very long life span. In Central America it is often used as a shade tree in coffee plantations. The fruit looks somewhat like a mango and is the size of an orange. It has a very thin skin which might be bright green or canary yellow. The flesh is a smooth pale yellow or white, custard-like pulp surrounding 2–5 large, flat seeds. The portion near the papery skin can be quite bitter. The best way to avoid biting into this is to cut the fruit in half and scoop the flesh out, making sure to avoid the pulp adjacent to the skin. If required, sprinkle a little sugar or a few drops of lime juice on the fruit.

The fruit quickly deteriorates after having been picked—changing from rock-like hardness to ripe-tenderness within three days. It is preferable to chill it before serving. Most varieties freeze well without any noticeable loss in taste.

CASIMIROA SOUFFLÉ

Ingredients:
120gm/4 egg whites
salt to taste
250gm/8oz casimiroa, peeled, seeded, mashed
10ml/2tsp lemon juice
20gm/1-1/2tbsp sugar

Method: Whip egg whites and salt till stiff. Add lemon juice and sugar to fruit pulp. Fold fruit into egg whites and transfer to a buttered dish. Bake at 180°C for 40 minutes, until the soufflé is firm in the centre. Serve hot or cold, as a dessert. Serves 2.

To preserve a casimiroa, scoop out the pulp and freeze in small containers. The thawed fruit can be used for drinks, as a sorbet or for sauces. Although the appearance might change, the taste does not.

Casimiroa has a mild, sweet flavour—which can have a hint of any one of many fruit—mango, coconut, lemon or peach.

DIMENSIONS:

fruit:
length: 30-70 cm
weight: 1.5-30 kg

SEASON:
all year round

PROPAGATION:
seeds

USES AS FOOD:
eaten fresh; used in salads, as juice—fresh and canned; dried seeds are eaten, also source for vegetable oil

OTHER USES:
as traditional Chinese medicine

Citrullus lanatus

WATERMELON

(Thai name: *tang-mo*)

Origin:
Africa

Distribution:
Throughout the tropics and subtropics

Varieties:
Numerous, differing in size, shape, colour of skin, flesh, and even the seeds. There are also seedless varieties

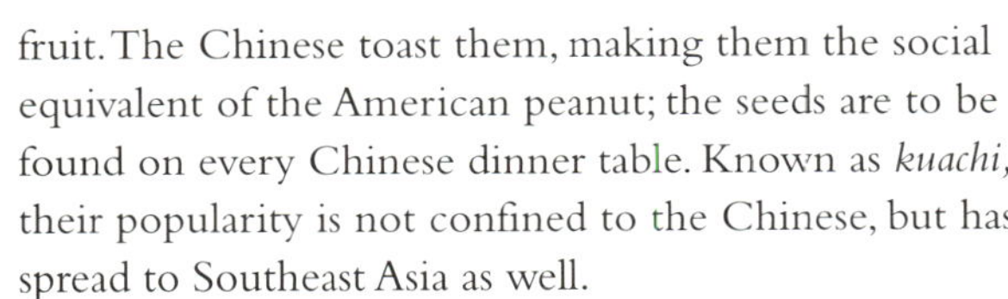

The seeds and skin of the watermelon are used in traditional medicine to treat numerous ailments. Cut off the skin, about 5 mm thick, and dry in the sun. Similarly, wash and dry the seeds in the sun. The skin is used in combination with wintermelon skin to treat diabetes. For nephritis it is mixed with Japanese raspberry root, and for patients suffering from high blood pressure, it is blended with gambir plant. The kernel of the seed is used, after removing the shell, for constipation in the aged and for weakness after childbirth.

This most ancient of fruits was well known to the ancient Egyptians, as bas reliefs and sculptures show that watermelons were grown in the Nile River valley in the time of the pharaohs. Linnaeus, the Swedish botanist, located their origin in central Italy, while another theory traces their origin to prehistoric times in India. Yet it took its time to spread further, probably because of the problem of passage. It only reached China, for instance—presumably via Southeast Asia—in the 10th century. The watermelon belongs to a large and distinguished family of vines, which includes gourds and cucumbers. While some are trained to climb, the watermelon, with its very large fruit, spreads across the ground.

The watermelon is very juicy, its flavour varying from the insipid to the slightly acidic and markedly sweet. It is a popular and refreshing fruit during the hot summers. Embedded in its deep pink or yellow flesh, which is protected by a thick green rind, are small dark brown or black edible seeds—some 200 to 900 in each fruit. The Chinese toast them, making them the social equivalent of the American peanut; the seeds are to be found on every Chinese dinner table. Known as *kuachi,* their popularity is not confined to the Chinese, but has spread to Southeast Asia as well.

The flesh contains glucose, fructose and sucrose, while the seeds contain oil, protein and vitamin B. The amount of oil varies from one species to another; some produce enough to make a useful cooking oil. The juice of the watermelon makes a refreshing drink, and is bottled and canned. The fruit also serves as a popular dessert fruit by itself and in combination with others.

The juice and flesh are considered useful in cases of heatstroke, fever, vomiting and general debility. It is also advised in related conditions of fever which leave the mouth dry with a bitter taste and bad breath. It is also known to cure complaints related to the urinary tract.

Signs of a good watermelon:

1. Firmness: It should be firm but not hard. Softness indicates that the fruit is overripe. Test the stem area in particular.

2. Heaviness: A heavy fruit is better as it indicates a higher water content.

3. Maturity: The underside of the melon should not be hard, white or very pale green. That means the fruit could be unripe.

One of the oldest, and most popular, ways of testing a watermelon is the 'tapping' or 'thumping' method.

Rap the fruit with the knuckles. The sound should be muffled. A hollow sound indicates it is either overripe, or immature.

DAMAR WULAN (*watermelon cocktail*)

Ingredients:
30ml/1oz Midori
10ml/2tsp vodka
60ml/1/4cup mango juice
120ml/1/2cup watermelon juice
120ml/1/2cup pineapple juice
topped with lemonade

Method: If using fresh fruit, make juice from fruit pulp in a blender and dilute with water. Put all ingredients in a cocktail shaker and shake to blend. Serve chilled in whole, scooped-out watermelon. Garnish with hibiscus or orchid. Serves 1.

Courtesy of *The Ritz-Carlton Bali*

DIMENSIONS:
tree:
height: up to 4.5 m
fruit:
diameter: 4–6 cm

SEASON:
perennial

PROPAGATION:
seeds; grafting

CULINARY USES:
as flavouring for food and drink

OTHER USES:
medicinal; industrial (flavouring) applications; citric acid

Citrus aurantifolia

LIME

(Thai name: *ma-now*)

Origin:
Southeast Asia

Distribution:
Predominantly in Southeast Asia, Italy, Spain, Mexico and West Indies

Varieties:
Innumerable, marked by differences in skin thickness, pith and juice

Lime juice is part of ritual washing ceremonies, such as during weddings, in India and Malaysia.

In traditional medicine, because of the lime's reputed antagonism to evil spirits which are believed to shy away from its presence, the witch doctor douses the patient to be exorcised with a jar of water filled with limes.

A Burmese proverb has its own version of 'putting the cart before the horse'. It recommends against searching for the lime before the hare is caught.

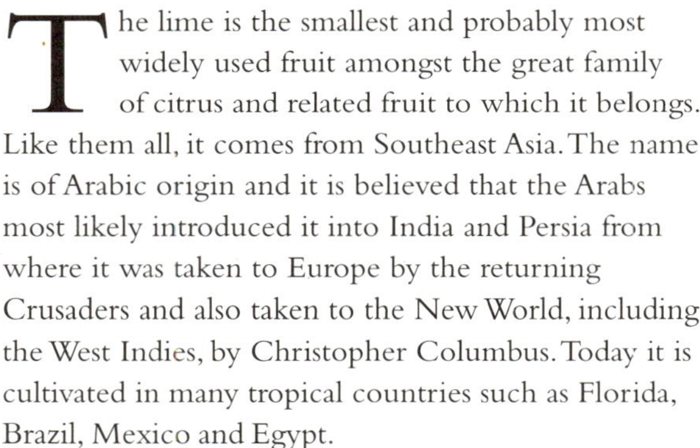

The lime is the smallest and probably most widely used fruit amongst the great family of citrus and related fruit to which it belongs. Like them all, it comes from Southeast Asia. The name is of Arabic origin and it is believed that the Arabs most likely introduced it into India and Persia from where it was taken to Europe by the returning Crusaders and also taken to the New World, including the West Indies, by Christopher Columbus. Today it is cultivated in many tropical countries such as Florida, Brazil, Mexico and Egypt.

Limes grow on thorned evergreen shrubs. The pulp tastes decidedly sour, and the fruit contains twice the amount of juice as the yellow, larger lemon. The juice, as a drink, makes one of the best thirst-quenchers. Lime cordials can be made at home and mixed with either water or soda water—adding both salt and sugar. The fruit itself primarily fulfils an important role as a flavouring for other foods, not being taken in its own right as it is far too tart and bitter for that. Sliced and squeezed, it offers piquancy to the papaya, adds tang to a fish dish or a curry, and gives pungency to a salad, a soup or a sauce. The zest, the outermost skin of the lime, is a valuable addition to a number of dishes and is included in the finely-grated form.

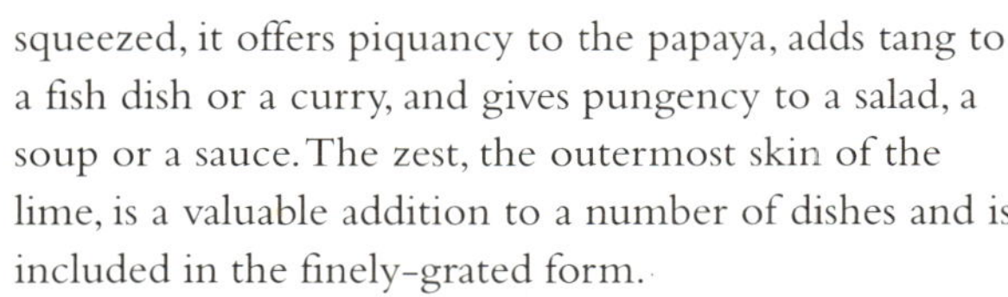

The acid content of lime is known to slow down the oxidation of fresh-cut fruits and vegetables, thus preventing discolouration and acting as a preservative.

Lime, because of its high vitamin C content, plays an auxiliary role in traditional medicine. A Malay book of medicine cites 29 different uses for it—ranging from headaches and neuralgia to dysentery, gonorrhoea and yaws. It is a pep-up in cases of listlessness and a rundown feeling due to vitamin deficiency. The pectin content in the fruit pulp is said to be beneficial in lowering blood cholesterol.

Lime lends its flavour to industrial preparations of herbal ointments and cosmetics, its oil is used in soaps and shampoos, and it provides a major source for citric acid. In short, it is virtually indispensable.

LIME MERINGUE TART

Shell
Ingredients:
450gm/150oz butter
226gm/1cup+2tbsp sugar
2 eggs
680gm/4-1/2cups cake flour

Meringue
200gm/6-7 egg whites
200gm/1cup sugar

Lemon filling
Ingredients:
3 whole eggs
3 egg yolks
226gm/1cup+2tbsp sugar 90ml/juice of 6 large limes
2tbsp lime zest from 2 large limes
90gm/3oz butter

Method: *Shell:* In a blender or bowl mix butter and sugar. Beat in the eggs. Stir in the flour, a little at a time, mixing well. Wrap dough in plastic and refrigerate for 2 hours until firm. Roll out the dough into circles to fit into tart pans with removable bottoms. Chill dough shell for 1 hour. Preheat oven to 200°C, line tart shells with wax paper and fill with dried beans. Bake for 15 minutes. Remove paper and beans and prick bottom with a fork. Cool to room temperature.

Lemon filling: In a pan combine all ingredients except butter over medium heat. Whisk until light and fluffy. Remove from the heat and whisk in butter. Pour into the prebaked shells and chill.

Meringue: Beat egg whites and sugar together until snow white and stiff. Pipe on top of Lime Tart. Bake for 10 minutes at 180°C. 'Spray' lighter flame on meringue to get charred effect. Serves 10–12.

Courtesy of *The Ritz-Carlton Hotel, Bali*

Pickled Lime: Take 500 gm of fresh lime in a glass or ceramic bowl or jar. Add 250 gm salt. Keep it exposed to the sun for a couple of days. The skin will turn brown, the fruit shrinks and will become dry and wrinkled. When properly dehydrated the fruit will keep for a long time, tasting better with age.

1 medium lime will give:
1-1/2 tbsp juice, and
1-1/2 tsp zest

To get more juice from a lime:
- *roll the fruit around on a table top with the palm of your hand, until it softens;*
- *soak dried, shrivelled limes in hot water for half an hour.*

Use a cut lime to remove:
- *onion and fish odours from your hands, knives and chopping board;*
- *turmeric and ink stains from your fingers and nails.*

DIMENSIONS:
tree:
height: up to 9 m

fruit:
diameter: 10–30 cm
weight: up to 1 kg

SEASON:
all the year round

PROPAGATION:
cuttings, marcotting, budding

CULINARY USES:
as a fruit; in salads

OTHER USES:
medicinal

Citrus grandis

POMELO/SHADDOCK

(Thai name: *som-o*)

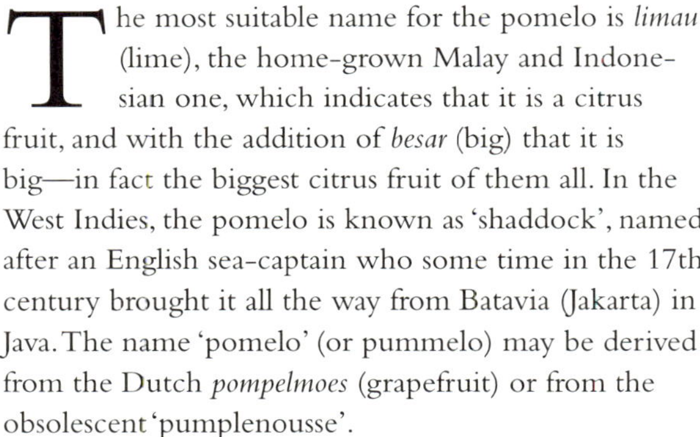

Origin:

Indonesia and Malaysia

Distribution:

Indonesia, Malaysia, South Asia, West Indies and New Zealand

Varieties:

Numerous, from the very acidic to the palatable; with seeds and seedless

The pomelo is believed to be the 'father' of the grapefruit and the 'mother' was perhaps the lemon. The hybrid grapefruit was first seen in Jamaica in the late 19th century.

Pomelo has a very high content of tannic acid, which stains clothes easily, and is difficult to remove.

The most suitable name for the pomelo is *limau* (lime), the home-grown Malay and Indonesian one, which indicates that it is a citrus fruit, and with the addition of *besar* (big) that it is big—in fact the biggest citrus fruit of them all. In the West Indies, the pomelo is known as 'shaddock', named after an English sea-captain who some time in the 17th century brought it all the way from Batavia (Jakarta) in Java. The name 'pomelo' (or pummelo) may be derived from the Dutch *pompelmoes* (grapefruit) or from the obsolescent 'pumplenousse'.

The pomelo resembles, on a large scale, all the characteristics of the grapefruit to which it is closely related. The yellow or reddish segments into which the former is divided are similar to those of the grapefruit but are more tightly packed together; likewise, the membrane which envelops them is tougher, and also the skin is thicker. In taste is the sweet-sourness of the yellow grapefruit more tart.

The grapefruit originated in the West Indies where it flourishes best, which means that it is younger than the pomelo and is rarely cultivated in Southeast Asia.

The fruit is low in calories and very high in vitamin C and potassium. The pomelo's prime function is as a fruit or in a salad. A sprinkling of sugar over the fruit enhances the flavour. The thick rind is gaining popularity as the basis for marmalade.

It is a favourite of the Chinese on occasions such as the new year and mooncake festival when it appears on altars before being ceremoniously consumed.

The pomelo has traditional medicinal uses. Both the Malays and the Filipinos use its leaves—the Malays to make a lotion to apply to sores and swellings, and the Filipinos as a sedative for certain nervous complaints. The Chinese also prepare medicaments from its leaves, fruit and flowers in combination with other ingredients. These cure indigestion, coughs, and car sickness. The fruit, if chewed slowly, is said to cure a hangover. A paste of pomelo rind and ginger applied to joints brings relief from rheumatic pains.

YUM SOM-O *(spicy pomelo salad with shrimp and coconut flakes)*

Salad
Ingredients:
350gm/2cups pomelo meat
120gm/1/2cup peeled,cooked prawns, sliced
35gm/1/4cup roasted ground peanuts
12gm/1/4cup roasted grated coconut
5gm/1tbsp fried sliced shallots
1 tsp/1 medium red chilli, thinly sliced
1 tsp/4 thinly sliced Kaffir lime leaves

Spicy sauce
Ingredients:
1 roasted dried red chilli
80gm/1cup roasted dried ground shrimp
100gm/1-1/3cups roasted shallot, sliced
60gm/3tbsp palm or brown sugar
45ml/3tbsp fish sauce
45ml/3tbsp tamarind juice

Method: Mix all ingredients of the salad, except red chilli and kaffir lime leaves. Pound or blend all dry ingredients of the sauce until thoroughly ground. Add fish sauce and tamarind juice and boil until thick. Cool. Pour sauce on the salad and mix well. Put in a dish and sprinkle with sliced red chilli and Kaffir lime leaves.

Courtesy of *Royal Orchid Sheraton Hotel & Towers, Bangkok*

The citrus is the only fruit that is neatly packaged. Its juicy pulp is arranged into neat, edible, crescent segments wrapped in a membrane which doubles as a partition. Between the segments and the fleshy skin—which can be either smooth or textured—strands and flesh wrapped around the segments further protect them.

To test for a ripe fruit, gently press the skin with a finger. It should pit slightly. The heavier the fruit the better. Another indication of a ripe pomelo is a rich aroma.

DIMENSIONS:

tree:
height: 20–30 m
dwarf variety: 9–12 m

fruit:
diameter: 20–30 cm

MATURITY:
5–6 years
dwarf: 4 years

SEASON:
all year round

LIFESPAN:
80–100 years

PRODUCTIVITY:
30 years

PROPAGATION:
fruit

CULINARY USES:
milk used in curries,
flesh used in desserts

OTHER USES:
numerous

The coconut, with its three 'eyes' is believed to represent Lord Siva, the three-eyed god of the Hindu Trinity.

Cocos nucifera

Coconut

(Thai name: *ma-phrao)*

Origin:
India, tropical Americas, Southeast Asia

Location:
Tropical lowlands below 500 m,
but most fertile in sandy, coastal areas

Varieties:
Numerous types depending upon fruit shape, size and husk.

The coconut is found throughout the tropical and equatorial regions. Generally taken for granted, the fruit is undoubtedly 'Nature's greatest gift to man'—and is often referred to as the 'tree of heaven'.

Coconut trees grow primarily near the sea, as they are able to tolerate the salt content along the sandy shores. The coconut is considered a lifesaver! Its kernel provides food and when dried (copra) yields oil with numerous traditional and modern applications. Its husk can be used as a fuel or to make coir matting. The fibres from its leaves are woven as clothing; the leaves are used for thatching and its timber for building. The hard shell of the coconut can form a cup, a ladle, or a measure (the Malay *cupak* = half a coconut scoop). In many parts of Southeast Asia, the birth of a child is marked by planting this tree of life. Coconut plays an important role in religious offerings and in many rituals connected with marriages, thanksgiving and childbirth, in the many countries where it grows. When embarking upon any new venture, Hindus first offer a coconut to the family deity before it is broken and the water from the nut is splashed on the idol. Pieces of the kernel are then distributed and eaten.

Being such a multipurpose fruit, the coconut has become an integral part of local cuisine. Its kernel, grated and squeezed, produces the cream (Malay *santan*) indispensable to all Southeast Asian curries. Boiled toddy (sap of the coconut palm inflorescence) results in a thick brown sugar (*gula melaka*), used for sweets and savouries. *Bibingka*, a favourite Philippine dish, consists of a mixture of ground rice, eggs, coconut milk and sugar cooked together over charcoal. Once set, it is topped with white cheese or salted duck eggs.

The coconut is considered a traditional antidote to poisoning and its parts, combined with certain local medicinal herbs, are seen as remedies for ailments. A concoction from the shell can kill insects and relieve itching. The flesh is known to relieve constipation. Coconut oil is widely used as a cosmetic for hair and skin in Southeast Asia.

In India, the full moon (purnima) during the months of July-August is celebrated as Narial Purnima (narial — coconut) by those who depend upon the sea for their livelihood. Coconuts are thrown into the sea as offerings to Varun the sea-god.

The name 'coconut' is thought to be derived from the Portuguese for monkey (quoque). The Portuguese travellers who brought the fruit back to Europe obviously saw a resemblance to a monkey's face in the 'hairy' ball with its three black 'eyes'.

COCONUT ICE CREAM

Ingredients:
500ml/2cups milk
250ml/2cups heavy cream
250ml/1cup coconut milk
8 egg yolks
250gm/1-1/4cups sugar
50gm/1cup desiccated coconut

Method: Beat egg yolks with sugar till frothy. Boil milk, cream and coconut milk together. Remove from stove and add to egg and sugar mixture, stirring constantly. Bring back to stove and heat up to 85°C. Take off the fire and strain. Add coconut. Cool over ice and freeze. Yields approximately 2 litre ice cream.

Courtesy of *Mandarin Singapore*

DIMENSIONS:
fruit:
weight: 1–15 kg

SEASON:
all year round

PRODUCTIVITY:
cultivated as an annual

PROPAGATION:
seeds

CULINARY USES:
eaten as a vegetable or cooked in sweet dishes

OTHER USES:
medicinal, oil for lamps

The seeds of the pumpkin, which are used extensively as Chinese home remedies, contain protein, and vitamins B_1, B_2 and C. The ailments the seeds are known to cure range from whooping cough in children to haemorrhoids, anaemia, lack of milk in nursing mothers, and tapeworms and roundworms in children .

Cucurbita pepo

PUMPKIN

(Thai name: *fuk-thong)*

Origin:

Mexico

Distribution:

Tropical lowlands up to 1500 m

The pumpkin remained in its Mexican homeland until the Spanish conquistadors arrived and exported it from the New World to the Old, along with other members of the same family such as the marrows, squash and the musk melon.

This globular fruit, which ranges in colour from shades of greens, deep golden-yellow or pale whitish-green, is eaten more as a vegetable, as part of the main meal. However, it is in reality, until properly attended to by the cookery experts, rather a prosaic and dull fruit. Nevertheless, it is a cook's delight and lends itself to many a delightful and imaginative combination. In addition to savoury dishes, pumpkin can also be used to flavour cakes and pies. Perhaps the most famous pumpkin dish is the American pumpkin pie traditionally served at Thanksgiving dinner.

Despite the thick flesh—there is not too much of it, in relation to its size—the centre of the pumpkin is hollow and the seeds are held in place by a mass of spongy fibres. The nutritious flesh has a high water and oil content. In its raw state, most people find it indigestible, and in some parts of the world it is considered (with no basis in actual fact) as dangerously poisonous.

The pumpkin can be used as a fodder. Its oil is also used as a fuel to light wicker lamps.

Sun-dried or roasted and salted pumpkin seeds are quite a popular snack in Mexico, the Americas, the Middle East, Southeast Asia and India. They are also used as substitutes for nuts. Health food shops sell the seeds unsalted and skinned and include them in muesli.

PUMPKIN BREAD PUDDING

Ingredients:
2 mini ripe pumpkins
(weighing 300gm/10oz each)
3 croissants
100gm/1/2cup sugar
15gm/1tbsp, heaped, sultanas
10gm/2 tsp melted butter
5 eggs
2 egg yolks
1/4tsp vanilla essence
250ml/1 cup milk
250ml/1cup cream (35% fat)
1/8tsp ground cinnamon
1/8tsp ground ginger

Method: Cut croissants into cubes. Divide into 2 equal portions. Cut off top of the pumpkins, scoop out seeds and steam pumpkin for 15 minutes. Turn pumpkin over to drain the moisture. Fill with croissant cubes and sultanas. Mix the remaining ingredients till well incorporated. Pour into pumpkins, leaving 1 cm from the top. Bake at 180°C for 40 minutes. To test whether mixture is cooked, insert a skewer into the custard. If it comes out clean, the custard is cooked. Serve hot. Serves 8.

Courtesy of *Le Meridien Singapore*

DIMENSIONS:
tree:
height: 10–20 m
fruit:
diameter: 1–3 cm

SEASON:
fruits twice a year: end of dry season and late summer

PROPAGATION:
budding, marcotting (the process of notching the stem of a plant and enveloping it in moist moss or soil, then cutting and potting the stem below the roots where these appear)

CULINARY USES:
eaten fresh and cooked; suitable for canning

OTHER USES:
medicinal (traditional)

A remedy for ringworm: take some kernels from the stones of the longan and grind to a paste with rice vinegar. Apply on the affected parts.

Dimocarpus longan

LONGAN

(Thai name: *lam-yai*)

Origin:
Southern China, Myanmar

Distribution:
Subtropical and tropical Southeast Asia

Varieties:
Numerous cultivated strains

A prolific bearer, the longan is also known as 'dragon's eye' (because of an ovoid, white eye-shaped mark on the pit) to distinguish it from its cousin, the mata kuching or 'cat's eye'. It has also been described as the little brother of the lychee, to which it is closely related.

The longan is China's gift to Southeast Asia, where it was brought by Chinese emigrants hundreds of years ago. Its main base nowadays is Thailand, where it is canned and exported and is the country's largest fruit export earner.

The evergreen longan tree has heavily foliaged branches with leathery leaves which have a glossy surface, and underneath are covered with minute hair. The flowers are pale yellow and hairy. The yellowish-brown, globular fruit droops in clusters. The juicy pulp, which is easily separated from its parchment-coloured shell, is white and translucent. Embedded in it is a large, shiny jet black seed. The fruit is sweet to taste and has a musky aroma. Though most frequently eaten fresh or from the can in which it floats in its own juice, the longan can also be cooked with delicious results. In general, the fruit is considered tastier than the lychee but it is not as juicy. It can be used instead of lychees or even cherries in fruit salads, sweet and sour dishes and as a garnish for cocktail drinks. Both the Javanese and the Chinese dry the fruit and then use it as a tea drink.

In traditional Chinese food therapy, the longan is said to have a beneficial effect on a number of ailments. It has been used as a stock remedy for sore eyes and is also known to be used for stomach ache, insomnia, amnesia, and dropsy and as an antidote for poison. The fruit is said to invigorate the heart and spleen, nourish the blood and have a calming effect on the nervous system. The longan is rich in vitamin C and high in fibre and protein content and also contains potassium and other minerals. A spoonful of longan tonic, made of equal quantities of longan flesh and sugar simmered in water till it is reduced to a thick consistency, is recommended twice a day. Dried leaves and flowers of the longan tree are sold in shops selling Chinese herbs.

SAVOURY STUFFED LONGAN

Ingredients:
2 cloves garlic
10gm/2tsp crushed coriander seeds
20ml/1tbsp+1tsp soy sauce
60gm/1/2cup lightly packed brown or palm sugar
vegetable oil for frying
125gm/4oz minced pork
1gm/1 chopped de-seeded chilli
50gm/1/4cup roasted, ground peanuts
6gm/3tbsp fresh coriander leaves
salt and pepper to taste
500gm/2cups longan* flesh

Method: Fry crushed garlic and coriander seeds in oil. When garlic is golden add all other ingredients except the longan. Cook and stir until the mixture is brown and fairly dry. Add longan. Continue to cook over low heat and mix well for about 2 minutes. Serve as an entrée, or hors d'oeuvre, or as a main course with steamed rice.

* substitute lychees, rambutans and pineapple cubes for longan.

To dry longan: soak the fruit in scalding hot water for several minutes. Remove and spread in the sun until dry. Remove skin and seed and dry the flesh again in the sun.

DIMENSIONS:

tree:
height: 10–33 m
fruit:
diameter: 8–10 cm

SEASON:
towards end of hot season

PROPAGATION:
seeds, grafting

CULINARY USES:
eaten fresh, as a dessert, for making drinks

OTHER USES:
for making wooden combs and utensils

The fruit has numerous names: one is velvet apple, or peach bloom in India. In Malaysia it is sagalat (scarlet fruit) or buah mentega (butterfruit). In the Philippines, where it got its name mabolo, it is also called kamagon which, in Spanish, is camagon.

Diospyros blancoi

MABOLO/BUTTERFRUIT

(Thai name: *ma-bo-lo*)

Origin:
Philippines

Distribution:
Humid tropical lowlands, mainly in the Philippines

Varieties:
Many cultivated varieties, distinguished by colour, taste and quantity of hair on the twigs and leaves

The mabolo is essentially a fruit of the Philippines. In those islands, where it is regarded as a staple fruit, it is found extensively and the tree frequently serves to provide shade along highways.

While the older leaves are dark green, the newer ones are showy, pale green or pink with silky hair. The small male flowers are found in clusters while the female flowers are solitary and are borne on separate trees. The attractive mabolo has a thin, brownish-marron skin coated with golden-brown hair. The fruit often grow in pairs or threes on opposite sides of a branch. The skin gives off a strong, unpleasant cheesy odour, but once it is removed, the fruit is quite odour-free and has a distinct, sweetish flavour.

However, despite all attempts to introduce it to other parts of the world, particularly during the 19th century when it was taken to the Dutch East Indies, the Malay Peninsula and the Royal Botanic Gardens at Kew in London, it failed to catch on—except in parts of Java in Indonesia and in Thailand, where it is cultivated extensively today.

The fruit should be peeled before eating as the skin is tough and papery and has a fuzz on its surface, besides its disagreeable cheese-like odour. To further rid the mabolo of the smell, it is suggested that the peeled fruit be refrigerated for a couple of hours before it is eaten.

The flesh can be sliced, seasoned with lime juice and eaten or served with other fresh fruit.

When cut into strips and fried in butter, the mabolo becomes crisp and is quite tasty as a vegetable and can be served with sausages, ham, or any other spicy meat.

The heartwood of the mabolo tree is streaked and mottled with dark grey or sometimes black. In the Philippines, it is carved into decorative hair combs which are in great demand.

The fruit is a good source of vitamin B, calcium and iron.

There are 4 to 8 brown, smooth, wedge-shaped seeds, about 4 cm long, arranged in a circle around the central core. Yet some varieties of the mabolo are completely seedless.

DIMENSIONS:

tree:
height: up to 6 m

fruit:
diameter: 6–12 cm

SEASON:
most of the year round

PROPAGATION:
seeds

CULINARY USES:
eaten as fruit; used to flavour pies and desserts

OTHER USES:
traditionally used as a narcotic to stupefy and catch fish

'Persimmon cake' is used in varying combinations as a traditional remedy for diarrhoea, haemorrhoids, lung infections and asthma. To make the 'cake': the fruit should be plucked when the skin starts turning yellow. Peel and discard the skin and place the fruit in the sun to dry, applying pressure frequently on each fruit to gradually flatten it. Continue drying the flattened fruit in the sun until a white frosting appears and covers the entire surface. This form is known as persimmon cake.

Diospyros kaki

PERSIMMON

(Thai name: *look-plub*)

Origin:
China or Japan

Distribution:
Tropical Americas, Southeast Asia and Australasia

Varieties:
Numerous, varying in size, shape and flavour, depending upon where they are grown

This striking, flame-orange, waxy fruit is similar to a tomato in shape and has four, large brown 'petals'—the calyx—at the stem end. The fruit gets its name from the Algonquin Indians who formerly lived along the St. Lawrence River of eastern Canada. They called the American variety (*Diospyros virginiana*), which grew locally, *pessemin* or *putchamin*.

It is advisable to remove the skin before eating the pulp which, too, is bright orange. The fruit has to be harvested with care, and not be allowed to ripen and fall from the tree, because this would bruise the very tender and soft fruit. Similarly, the thin skin of ripe fruit is likely to disintegrate on being peeled. One way of overcoming this hazard is to freeze the whole fruit, and then, having thawed its exterior under running water, scrape off the skin.

Eating the fruit is still the best way of consuming it despite there being an abundance of recipes suggesting its inclusion in cakes, desserts, pies and ice cream. To preserve the ripe fruit, wrap it individually and freeze. When thawed it can be used in used in recipes as indicated. The persimmon, though high in calories, is very rich in vitamin A, fibre and potassium content.

The inhabitants of the West Indies traditionally augmented their supply of fish by exploiting the narcotic content of the persimmon. The pounded fruit cast into the water stupefies the fish, enabling them to be caught easily.

A traditional Chinese remedy for hiccups that will not stop: Take 9 grams of calyx of the persimmon fruit and 3 grams of fresh ginger. Add water and steam for a few minutes and eat. Alternately, take 3 grams of the calyx and stir-fry till fragrant. Crush and add to a spoonful of rice wine and drink.

PERSIMMON COCONUT MOUSSE

Ingredients:
250gm/1cup persimmon
100gm/1/2cup sugar
125ml/1/2cup sour cream
40gm/3/4cup grated coconut

Method:
Peel the persimmon. Blend flesh to form pulp. Add the other ingredients and mix. Serve chilled. Serves 2.

Durio zibethinus

DURIAN

(Thai name: *tu-rian*)

Origin:
Borneo (probably)

Distribution:
Indonesia, Malaysia, Isthmus of Kra (Thailand) and Tenasserim (south Myanmar)

Varieties:
Numerous, with the thickness of the pulp varying

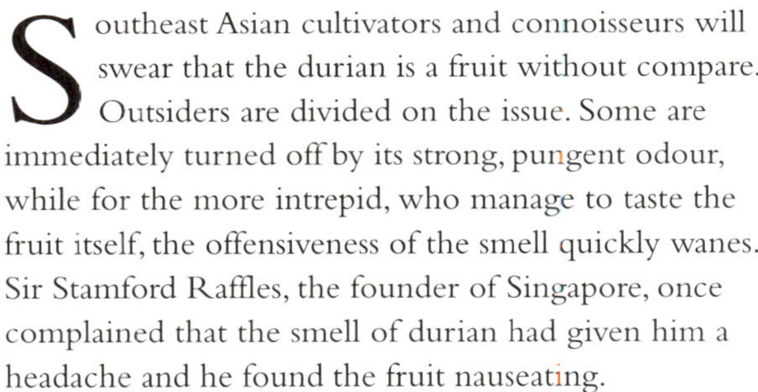

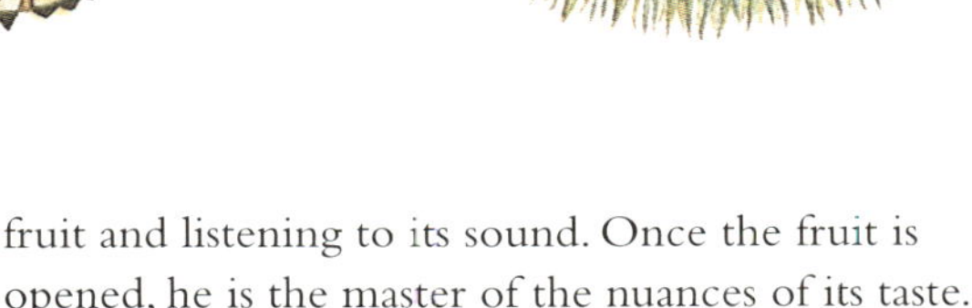

DIMENSIONS:
tree:
height: up to 27 m
fruit:
length: 20–35 cm
diameter: 18–22 cm
weight: 1–9 kg

SEASON:
varies according to location; usually biannual, though one season bears the bumper crop

PROPAGATION:
seeds, grafting, budding

CULINARY USES:
eaten fresh; used for making durian cake and paste; seeds also edible, boiled or roasted

OTHER USES:
medicinal

Each fruit is hung on a peduncle which, depending upon the variety, may be either long or short. This, in turn, is strongly attached to the branch or trunk.

Southeast Asian cultivators and connoisseurs will swear that the durian is a fruit without compare. Outsiders are divided on the issue. Some are immediately turned off by its strong, pungent odour, while for the more intrepid, who manage to taste the fruit itself, the offensiveness of the smell quickly wanes. Sir Stamford Raffles, the founder of Singapore, once complained that the smell of durian had given him a headache and he found the fruit nauseating.

Novelist Anthony Burgess, in his novel *Time for a Tiger*, describes the durian thus: 'like eating a sweet raspberry blancmange in a lavatory'. The odour is indeed so strong and pervasive that the best hotels refuse to allow their guests to bring durians into their rooms. But the proof is in the eating, and most people who partake of it become lifelong addicts.

The lore and art associated with its cultivation and the experience required to assess its qualities impart to the local durian connoisseur something of the aura of the wine taster of the West. He can determine the ripeness and quality of the inner pulp by shaking the fruit and listening to its sound. Once the fruit is opened, he is the master of the nuances of its taste.

Durians are not plucked but allowed to fall, which is when they are best for eating. The edible pulp enveloping its seeds is thick, yellowish and of a custard-like consistency. Rich in vitamins B, C and E and with a high iron content, the fruit is extremely nutritious; hence its reputation as an aphrodisiac. From fermented durian comes *tempoyak*, a popular Malay paste used with other condiments as a side dish. In Thailand, where durian production is highly commercialised, one finds a sybaritic mixture of durian, glutinous rice and peaches. *Dodol*, a traditional sweetmeat made from durian pulp cooked with sugar, is always available in the market place, and durian-flavoured ice cream has also become popular.

The high price of durian does not inhibit sales of this well-loved fruit, and a good crop can bring lucrative returns to orchard owners.

A preparation from its roots and leaves is prescribed by traditional doctors for fevers and jaundice.

DURIAN MOUSSE CAKE

Vanilla sponge

Ingredients:

10 whole large eggs
175gm/1cup+2tbsp flour
12gm/2 tsp cornflour
190gm/1cup sugar
6gm/2oz butter
25ml/5 tsp water

Method: Sieve flour and cornflour. Melt butter with warm water. Beat eggs and sugar until white and foamy. Fold in flour and add butter. Place mixture in cake tin and bake at 200°C for 15 minutes. Cool and slice the cake, horizontally, into three layers.

Durian mousse

200gm/1cup durian, puréed
25gm/2tbsp sugar
30ml/2tbsp water
65ml/1/4cup coconut milk
7gm/7 leaves gelatine
125ml/1/2cup single, fresh cream
150ml/3/5cup whipped cream

Method: Bring to boil durian purée, sugar, water and coconut milk. Add gelatine while stirring and set aside to cool. Add single and whipped cream. Spread mousse on the two lower layers of the cake and sandwich all three layers together. Cover the cake with cream and decorate with durian *dodol* (available in the market) and white chocolate shavings.

Courtesy of *Penang Mutiara Beach Resort, Penang, Malaysia*

To test a durian by its smell—balance it gingerly on one hand as its 'duri' (thorns) are sharp. Use the other hand as a funnel to direct the scent to the nose. Inhale deeply. Study the sky and look wise!

The creamy yellow flower opens in the afternoon, but falls off in the early morning, giving off an odour of sour milk.

DIMENSIONS:

tree:
height: 4–6 cm
fruit:
diameter: 4–6 cm
weight: 70–120 gm

SEASON:
2 or 3 harvests a year after dry season

PRODUCTIVITY:
up to 50 years

PROPAGATION:
seeds, grafting

CULINARY USES:
taken as a fruit

OTHER USES:
medicinal; as a timber; used in dyeing

Garcinia mangostana

MANGOSTEEN

(Thai name: *mung-kood)*

Origin:
Malaysia, Thailand and Indonesia

Distribution:
Humid tropical lowlands up to 500 m but confined to Southeast Asia

Varieties:
One only, but various strains

'The Manges Tanges contains four kernels, which melt like butter on the tonge and of so fine and refreshing a taste that I have never met with any fruit comparable to it. It is generally served up at the greatest Tables as the most delicious dish that can be made; drest with Sugar and Spice and put into fine China Dishes.'.
— Christopher Fryke, 17th century.

By popular acclaim, the mangosteen is held to be the most delectable of all tropical fruit, and has been proclaimed their queen—the durian vying with the mango for the title of the king. This relationship goes beyond mere titles, because it is common wisdom to take the 'cooling' mangosteen after eating the 'heaty' durian. The perfect couple!

The mangosteen is a beautiful evergreen fruit tree with its compact conical shape and shiny green leaves, but takes between 8 to 15 years to mature. It is dioecious, that means it has separate male and female trees, but the male plant is rarely found and the female plant appears to propagate itself through a kind of hermaphoditic process. The cultivated mangosteen reproduces by parthenogenesis, which means that the fruit is produced without fertilization.

The globular mangosteen is very delicate and easily bruised so that it has proved almost impossible to export to other tropical areas and remains confined to its Southeast Asian homeland.

However, there is no doubt about the luxury of its taste. It has won unstinted praise down the ages from all who have encountered it. The fruit has a thick, purplish-brown, leathery, shell-like exterior with the inner surface being pinkish-brown. There are four large, green sepals around the stem. Contained inside the rind is the juicy, soft, snow white pulp divided into five, six or more segments. These correspond to the number of flat woody lobes at the apex of the outer skin. The flavour is deliciously sweet.

The mangosteen has medicinal properties and is used in folk medicine in Southeast Asia. The fruit's rind, dried and sliced, is used as an astringent, and from it the people of Malaysia make a decoction for dysentery. The bark and the skin are also used as a cure for diarrhoea and to control fever. Its leaves, with a mixture of unripe bananas and a little benzoin, form a traditional balm for wounds, and the liquid from its boiled roots is reputed to aid irregular menstruation.

The rind, which contains a high content of tannin, is used to cure leather in Asia and as a mordant to fix the colour black in textile dyeing.

CHILLED MANGOSTEEN SAGO SOUP WITH DOM PERIGNON

Ingredients:
500gm/2cups mangosteen purée (from approx. 20 mangosteens)
100gm/1cup sugar
150ml/2/3cup water
300ml/1-1/4 cups Dom Perignon
250gm/1cup cooked sago
45ml/3tbsp lemon juice
45ml/3tbsp orange juice

Method: Boil sugar and water to form a syrup. Set aside to cool. Purée the mangosteen flesh and sieve to get juice. Wash sago repeatedly until water is clear. Boil water, add sago and cook till crystal transparent. Drain water from sago through a sieve. Place sago in ice water, drain again and set aside. Mix together mangosteen juice, orange juice, lemon juice, sugar syrup and cooked sago. Chill. Pour Dom Perignon, other champagnes into the mixture and stir well. Serve chilled.

Courtesy of *The Ritz Carlton Millenia, Singapore*

It is recorded that the flavour of the mangosteen found such great favour with the Queen-Empress Victoria that she is said to have offered a prize to whosoever succeed in bringing the fruit to England, without deterioration'.

DIMENSIONS:
tree:
height: 15–20 m
fruit:
duku—round
diameter: 5 cm
langsat—oval
diameter: 3–4 cm

SEASON:
fruits twice a year

PROPAGATION:
seeds

CULINARY USES:
eaten raw as fruit

OTHER USES:
medicinal; as an aromatic mosquito repellent

Langsat grows mainly in northern Malaysia, while the duku is found predominantly in the southern part of the peninsula, and in Indonesia.

Both langsat and duku have medicinal uses. Their skin, when burned, gives off a pleasant aroma and is reputed to be an effective mosquito repellent. The seeds of the langsat are said to be effective in removing intestinal worms and lowering fever, and the powdered bark is used as an antidote to the deadly sting of a scorpion.

Lansium domesticum

Duku and Langsat

(Thai name: *long-kong* and *lang-sart)*

Origin:
Indonesia and Malaysia

Distribution:
Tropical region, up to 800 m

Varieties:
Numerous depending upon thickness of skin and size of seed; and the cultivated and wild varieties

These two fruits are commonly known by the Malay names *duku* and *langsat* and belong to the langsat group. The flowers are small, stalkless and sweetly scented. The fruit grows in compact bunches of between 10 and 40 globular fruit. The similarity of the fruit, which lies in the colour of their patchy yellowish skins, and in their general shape and appearance, is enough to confuse any one unfamiliar with them. They also taste very similar.

Yet, in fact they are quite distinct from one another. The duku, the larger of the two, is rounder and has thicker skin which peels easily from the white or pale pink flesh within and contains no milky fluid, unlike the langsat. The fruit of the duku is made up of five unequal segments, some of which may contain a large thick seed that tastes very bitter. The fruit of the langsat is slightly ovoid. Of the two, the duku is generally the preferred fruit.

The duku and langsat have long been cultivated in Malaysia and Indonesia, and centuries ago acquired a high reputation among visitors, particularly those from China. In season, they regularly appear on roadside stalls near the orchards where they are grown, as well as in markets, attracting a good custom. A third member of the species (called *dokong* in Malaysia and *longkong* in Thailand), bigger and sweeter than duku, is also being cultivated and commands a high price in the market. The limitation of all these fruit lies in the fact that they can only be eaten as fresh fruit.

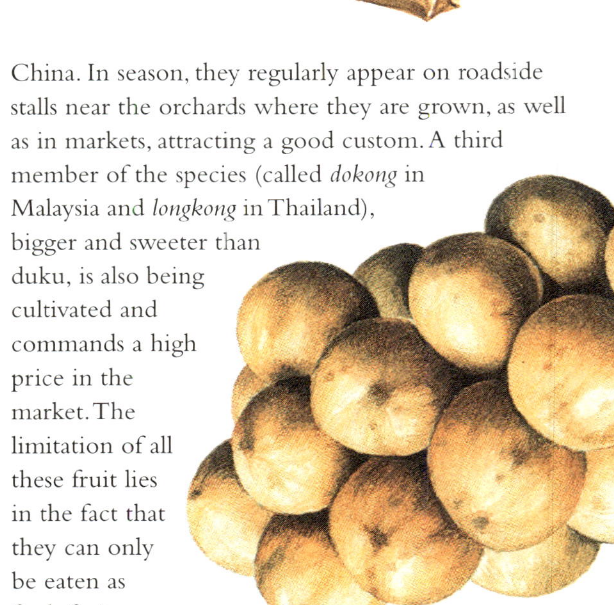

In the 15th century, Chinese voyagers saw duku and langsat trees in villages in Java. They took the seeds back and tried to cultivate them in China, but the trees could withstand neither the cold, nor the long dry spells.

Bats are the common pests that destroy the fruit. A little prawn paste (locally called belachan) is mixed with wet flour, tied in a piece of cloth, and hung on the trees. The strong smell keeps the bats away at night.

Litchi chinensis

LYCHEE

(Thai name: *lin-chee*)

Origin:
Southern China, Vietnam

Distribution:
Southern China;
tropical highlands

Varieties:
Numerous cultivated variants

DIMENSIONS:
tree:
height: up to 10 m
fruit:
diameter: 3 cm

SEASON:
early dry season

PROPAGATION:
marcotting, budding, cuttings

CULINARY USES:
eaten fresh as fruit; canned; used for flavouring

OTHER USES:
medicinal

In 1059, Chinese scholar Tsai Hsiang mentioned the lychee in what is considered to be the first published work on the fruit.

This is a member of the Sapindaceae family, which includes the longan, rambutan and pulasan. The name is derived from the Chinese word *lee chee* which means 'one who gives the pleasures of life'.

Though it is now grown in tropical uplands all over the world and its canned fruit is marketed almost everywhere, the lychee with its distinctive sweet taste and fragrance was slow to emerge from its Chinese homeland, where it is known to have been cultivated for over 4,000 years. Another theory has the fruit originating in the ancient kingdom of Annam, which is now central Vietnam. It did not penetrate the Southeast Asian mainland until the 17th century and it took another hundred years to reach India, which today is the world's largest producer of the canned fruit. The lychee reaached Australasia and the West Indies a century later.

The canned product appeared in the world market after 1945. Before that, lychees were known beyond the areas of its natural cultivation only in the form of lychee nuts—the sun-dried fruit, within their shells, with the appearance of raisins and the taste of dates.

The exotic lychee still retains something of its sybaritic reputation. In Honolulu where it is eaten as an appetizer, lychee is served in various combinations. A dish of lychees coated in chocolate sauce on ice cream is categorized as 'absolutely decadent'!

Lychees grow in clusters, which are picked in entirety with the stalk, when the skin of the fruit has changed colour from green to red. The fruit, which deteriorates quickly once harvested, is usually sold still attached to the stalk. Lychees consist of translucent, white pulp enveloping a single, brown seed encased in a red shell which easily peels. The flesh is relished fresh and used to flavour jellies, ice creams and sherbets. Usually, the lychee is opened by tearing the skin at the stem end, while experienced lychee eaters bite lightly through the skin in the upper half of the fruit and then squeeze the fruit out. The Chinese use the fruit for medicinal purposes and for making wine.

LYCHEE DUMPLINGS WITH PINEAPPLE SAUCE

Dumplings:
Ingredients:
12 fresh lychees, peeled and de-seeded
500gm/1lb potatoes baked and peeled
125gm/4oz butter (softened)
50gm/1/3cup semolina
1 whole egg
7gm/1/2tbsp salt
100gm/2/3cup flour
100gm/2cups palm or brown sugar
100gm/2cups grated coconut
few drops red food colouring
icing sugar and mint leaves for garnish

Method: Mash and put potatoes in a bowl. Make a well in the centre. Add butter, semolina, 1/2 egg white, egg yolk, salt. Mix well. Sift flour into mixture. Knead into smooth dough and chill for 15 minutes. Fill lychee cavities with brown sugar made wet with a little water. Roll out dough 3 mm thick on a floured board. Cut into 12 10-cm squares. Put stuffed lychee on each square and fold over corners to form a triangle. Seal edges. Boil water with salt. Lower dumplings gently and poach for about 15 minutes until they rise to the surface. Remove with a slotted spoon and refresh in cold water. Heat remaining butter in a pan. Add grated coconut and a few drops of food colouring. Toast coconut until crisp. Roll dumplings in coconut and sprinkle on icing sugar. Garnish with mint.

Sauce:
Ingredients:
15gm/1tbsp, heaped, cornflour or cornstarch
20ml/4tbsp Kirsch
50gm/1/2cup sugar
400ml/1-2/3 cups pineapple juice
100gm/1/2cup crushed pineapple

Method: Dissolve cornflour in Kirsch. Bring pineapple juice, sugar and cornflour mixture to a boil and stir continuously until thick. Add crushed pineapple. Serve with dumplings.

Courtesy of *New World Emperor Hotel Macau*

According to Dai Yin-fang and Liu Cheng-jun's book Fruits as Medicine, 'the nature of the flesh (of the lychee) is warm and it can help improve the blood. The flavour of the kernel is bitter-sweet and its nature is warm and it can help regulate the flow of vital energy, disperse the accumulation of evils' and ease pain.

In China, the lychee is known as the Fruit of Romance. For did not Emperor Hsuan Tsung try to capture the heart of the beautiful lady Yang Kuei Fei by sending her a basketful of the freshest—and juiciest—lychees by express pony?

Mangifera indica

MANGO

(Thai name: *ma-muang*)

DIMENSIONS:
tree:
height: up to 30 m
fruit:
length: 5–15 cm
diameter: 3–15 cm
weight: 30–800 gm

SEASON:
middle of the dry, hot season

PRODUCTIVITY:
up to 50 years

PROPAGATION:
budding, grafting, marcotting

CULINARY USES:
taken fresh and in desserts, ice creams, drinks and prepared as chutney and pickle

OTHER USES:
medicinal (leaves); boat building (timber)

Origin:

India and Southeast Asia

Distribution:

Tropical lowland, dry areas up to 300 m

Varieties:

Over 200, varying in size, flavour and weight

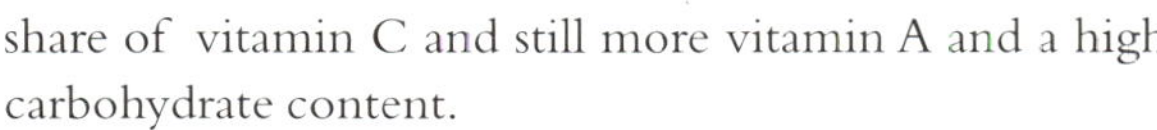

The 'king of fruits' is one of the most widely cultivated and, therefore, best known of tropical fruits. It is also the most highly consumed fruit in the world—more than either apples or bananas. The flavour of the mango can range from the banal to the sublime. Its season is most opportune just when the weather is at its driest and hottest and one's thirst most needs quenching. The fruit is a native of India and of Southeast Asia. The Malay/Indonesian name most commonly used, *mangga*, is actually a Sundanese (West Javanese) word applied to the wild fruit found in the jungle. Another Malay/Indonesian name, *mempelam*, is derived from Tamil which comes from the original in Sanskrit—*maha pahala* or 'great fruit'. This is also indicative of where the first cultivated mangoes came from over 4,000 years ago. The fruit was spread beyond South and Southeast Asia by the Portuguese and Spaniards, who carried it to tropical Africa, South America and the Pacific Ocean, especially to the islands of Hawaii.

The mango is one of the most nutritious fruits. With a high (16 per cent) sugar content, it has a fair share of vitamin C and still more vitamin A and a high carbohydrate content.

Its soft, succulent fruit, housed in a thin green, yellowish or even reddish-pink skin, envelops a shell which protects the seed inside from all but the sharpest of (monkeys') teeth. The best varieties are excellent even when eaten fresh, with the consistency and flavour of the best peaches; while others can be tart or pungent to the palate. The ripe fruit goes well in all sorts of combinations. Its juice makes an excellent drink, often canned for export. It flavours ice creams and sherbets, cereals, baby foods and fruit bars. It makes excellent pickle and chutney, and its pectin content enables it to serve as a setting agent for jellies and jams.

The rest of the tree also has its uses. Its leaves have various applications in the traditional medicines of India and Southeast Asia. In India, it also serves as green fodder for cattle, though only in the absence of normal fodder, for too much of such fare makes the cattle ill. The timber of the mango tree is stout and beetle-resistant, so that it has been a preferred wood for boat building, especially for canoes and dugouts.

To the Moghul Emperor Akbar goes the credit for popularizing the mango in India. During his reign, in the late 16th century, he had 100,000 mango trees planted across northern India.

CHAMPAGNE MANGO CAKE

Sponge Fingers:
Ingredients:
720gm/24 egg whites
440gm/4cups castor sugar
400gm/14 egg yolks
200gm/1-1/4cups cornflour
200gm/1-1/4cups flour

Method: Beat egg white and add sugar. Sift flour and cornflour together into a bowl. Add yolks to egg white and then the flour and mix gently. Pour the mixture 1 cm thick on baking tray and spread evenly. Bake at 170°C for about 25 minutes. Cool sponge and cut into thin slices.

Champagne Mousse
500ml/2cups champagne
350ml/1-2/5cups sugar syrup (boil sugar with water)
280gm/10 egg yolks, whipped
700ml/2-3/4cups whipping cream
12 gelatine leaves, soaked in ice cold water
zest of 1/2 orange
1–2 ripe mangoes peeled, cubed

Method: Pour syrup over yolks and whip till cool. Squeeze water from gelatine and dissolve in a little champagne. Add rest of champagne. Add all ingredients to whipped cream. Line the bottom and sides of a 20-cm ring cake tin with a layer of sponge. Cover with mango. Pour in 3/4th of the mousse. Repeat layer of sponge and mousse. Refrigerate. Serve chilled.

Courtesy of *Singapore Marriott Hotel*

In India, the mango is revered by Hindus. Legend has it that the daughter of the Sun ran away from a wicked sorceress and later emerged from the seed of the mango.

In the sub-continent, too, a variety of the mango is commonly eaten without it being cut! The fruit is gently squeezed to liquefy the pulp, then a hole is made at the top where it joins the stem, and the pulp is sucked and squeezed out simultaneously by continuously kneading it. Care must be taken that the skin doesn't split during this process.

DIMENSIONS:
tree:
height: 9–12 m
fruit:
diameter: 5–10 cm
weight: 80–120 gm

SEASON:
all the year round

PROPAGATION:
marcotting, budding, seeds

CULINARY USES:
as a fruit; source of chewing gum

OTHER USES:
medicinal; as a hardwood; tanning

Manilkara zapota

SAPODILLA

(Thai name: *la-mood)*

Origin:
Central America

Distribution:
Throughout the humid tropics

Varieties:
3 major wild varieties; 2 major cultivated varieties

It is believed that once there were over 100 million sapodilla trees in Central America's northeast Guatemala and Belize alone. Today, coastal India is the largest producer of sapodilla.

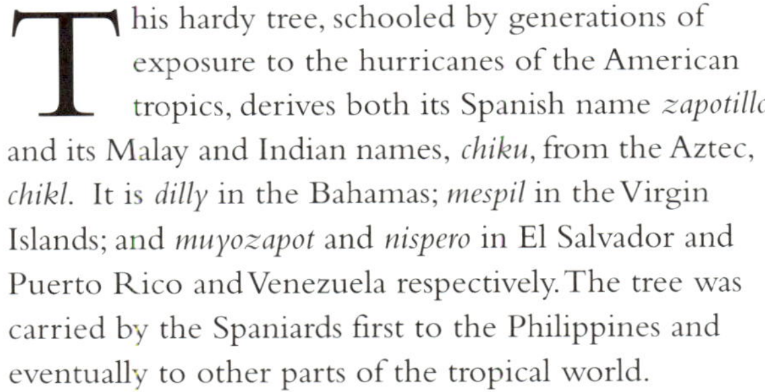

This hardy tree, schooled by generations of exposure to the hurricanes of the American tropics, derives both its Spanish name *zapotillo* and its Malay and Indian names, *chiku*, from the Aztec, *chikl*. It is *dilly* in the Bahamas; *mespil* in the Virgin Islands; and *muyozapot* and *nispero* in El Salvador and Puerto Rico and Venezuela respectively. The tree was carried by the Spaniards first to the Philippines and eventually to other parts of the tropical world.

In most tropical regions, the tree is valued primarily for its fruit. It grows slowly and is distinctly pyramidal when young with ornamental glossy leaves. The flowers are small and bell-like. It fruits prolifically—bearing an average of 3,000 fruit a year. These are small, round or oval fruit with smooth brown skin which is coated with a pale brown scurf when unripe. The flesh is soft, pulpy, with a granular texture, yet is delicate and pleasing to the palate. The black, hard, glossy seeds have a white line on the side and a distinct curved hook on one edge. To capture the full flavour, the fruit must be eaten as soon as it is ripe. Though the sapodilla is transportable, it bruises easily and cannot be processed.

In the Americas, the milky sap of the sapodilla tree is the main ingredient in the manufacture of chewing gum which gives the tree its main importance there. The Spaniards learned the secret of preparing the gum, *chicle*, from the Aztec, who tapped the bark for its sap which they then boiled, the gum separating itself in the process. Modern industrialization has done the rest.

The Aztec and the Maya of Mexico valued the sapodilla for its hard, heavy wood which they used for their homes. The proof of its durability can be seen in the well-preserved ruins of the Mayan cities of Yucatan, abandoned some 600 years ago.

Sapodilla is increasingly being used as a flavouring for ice creams and desserts. It has a high tannin content which makes it useful as a source for dyes. In traditional medicine its juice can also be applied as a purgative and as a remedy for diarrhoea. A decoction of the yellowed leaves is drunk as a remedy for coughs and colds. A liquid extracted from crushed seeds is used as a diuretic and is found to be effective in removing kidney and bladder stones, while a paste from the seeds is useful for treating venomous stings and bites.

You can make sapodilla pie in the same way you do an apple pie. Line a pie dish with uncooked pie crust. Fill it with sapodilla slices and raisins. Pour in 1/2 cup lemon or lime juice (to prevent the fruit from turning rubbery), and sprinkle half a cup of sugar. Cover with another layer of pie crust and seal the edges. Make slits with a knife, or pierce holes with a fork, on the crust to allow steam to escape. Bake in hot oven (350°F/175°C) for 30 to 40 minutes.

CHIKU AUR LASOON KI KHEER **(*sapodilla milk pudding with garlic*)**

Ingredients:
4 sapodilla (*chiku*)
100gm/1cup garlic cloves, peeled and sliced thinly
11/4cups milk
100gm/1/2cup sugar
5ml/1tsp rose water
pinch of alum
2.5gm/1/2tsp powdered cardamom

Method: Peel and de-seed sapodilla and blend with a little milk to form a thick purée. Boil water, add alum and garlic, boiling for another 10 minutes. Drain and wash. Change water and repeat twice more. Remove garlic and set aside to cool. Boil milk in a heavy bottomed pan, stirring constantly till it thickens and is reduced to 1/4 its quantity. Add sugar and cardamom and cook for another 5 minutes. Remove and cool. Add garlic and sapodilla and cook for another five minutes. Remove, add rosewater. Cool and serve chilled.

Courtesy of *Ramada Hotel Manohar, Hyderabad, India*

DIMENSIONS:

plant:
height 4–9 m
(according to species)

fruit:
length: 8-20 cm
diameter: 2-5 cm
weight: 50–200 gm

SEASON:
all year round

PRODUCTIVITY:
10-14 months

PROPAGATION:
suckers (shoots spring from underground stem or corm)

CULINARY USES:
eaten fresh; cooked in many combinations

OTHER USES
medicament, as utensils (leaves)

'The leaves are so large that one of them will shelter a man from the Sun and Rain ...'
— Christopher Fryke, ship's surgeon, 17th century

Musa spp.

BANANA

(Thai name: *kluay*)

Origin:
Southeast Asia

Distribution:
Tropics and subtropics below 1200 m, worldwide

Varieties:
Numerous—best for eating: *Musa paradisica;* best for cooking: *Musa sapientium* (plantain)

The name banana is taken from a local name of the plant in Guinea (Africa). In Europe and North America, where it is probably the most familiar of all tropical fruits, it does not come from its original Southeast Asian home but from the plantations of Central America and Brazil. In fact, it is one of the few tropical plants to have travelled westwards to the Americas, via India, Africa and Arabia, instead of the other way around. Yet its place of origin in the Old World is hard to determine, though it is mentioned in ancient Greek texts and Alexander the Great mentions having seen the fruit in India.

The Arabs called it 'Tree of Paradise', but it is not a tree. It is a large herb. Its trunk is a mesh of intertwining leaves, with the stem pushing up through the middle. Its large leaves often end up as primitive umbrellas. It is common practice in many Indian restaurants to serve take-away meals in a folded banana leaf which, when opened, doubles as the plate.

The earliest reference to this fruit goes back 2,500 years with the oldest written reference to it mentioning India. Its origin and rich nutrients have given the banana religious associations. The plant is, therefore, often found near temples, and figures in folklore as the abode of guardian spirits. Christians in the Middle Ages called the banana *Pomum paradisi* as they believed this, and not the apple, was the forbidden fruit with which the serpent made Eve tempt Adam.

The fruit is generally eaten uncooked, but is also prepared in numerous succulent ways. The Thai *klu-ai kai* which envelops the banana in a mixture of glutinous rice and flour. In Malaysia, *goreng pisang* (banana fritter) is a popular standby for any occasion. A dish of bananas cooked in a thick, spicy fish sauce and served with rice noodles is called *mohinga* and is claimed to have been a favourite dish of the former royal family of Burma (Myanmar).

The fibres from the leaves of a wild species, *Musa textilis*, produce abaca or Manila hemp.

The banana is considered an antidote to snake bites and as an effective treatment for blistered skin. Among certain people the fluid from its trunk is regarded as a cure-all for baldness.

In Thailand during the Loy Kratong festival little boats called kratong are made from banana stems and decorated with banana leaves. These are floated downstream, bearing the ills and regrets of the previous year.

BANANA AND WHITE CHOCOLATE MOUSSE

Ingredients:
600gm/3cups sugar
600gm/20 eggs
2kg banana, puréed
200ml/4/5cup lemon juice
36 gelatine leaves soaked in cold water
600gm/1-1/4cups white chocolate, melted and dissolved with gelatine
2l whipping cream

Method: Whisk sugar and eggs until smooth. Mix in banana. Add chocolate and set partially. Blend in cream and lemon juice. Set in mould by chilling. Remove. Serve with Chocolate Rum sauce.

Courtesy of *Courtyard by Marriott Great Barrier Reef, Cairns.*

DIMENSIONS:
tree:
height: up to 24 m
fruit:
diameter: 2.5–3.5 cm
weight: 25–40 gm
SEASON:
usually two crops a year, following dry spell
PRODUCTIVITY:
up to 50 years
PROPAGATION:
budding, marcotting
CULINARY USES:
as fresh fruit; canned; fruit juice and syrup
OTHER USES:
medicinal

Nephelium lappaceum

RAMBUTAN

(Thai name: *ngaw*)

Origin:
Indonesia, Malaysia

Distribution:
Humid, tropical lowlands up to 600 m

Varieties:
Wide range reflected in sweetness, thickness and juice content

Lappaceum, the scientific Latin name of the fruit, refers to its resemblance to a burr.

Some rambutan aficionados swear that the pulp tastes like both grapes and lemons.

The rambutan, a cousin of the Chinese lychee, owes its name to its hairy skin (*rambut* means 'hair' in Malay). It is a delicious and very popular fruit in Southeast Asia and Australia. However, it has hardly travelled outside the region, although it was carried by early Arab traders to as far as Zanzibar in East Africa where the tree is also cultivated. It is found in speciality shops in the West.

The fruit hang together in clusters on the ever-green trees. The tough, parchment-like skin with its soft, fleshy spikes (yet the skin is not prickly) turns a bright red, or in some cases has a yellowish hue, when ripe. Inside is the pearl-white, succulent pulp which has a sweet-sour taste. It encloses a long, hard, inedible seed. The seedcase is normally found sticking to the flesh. The ease with which the flesh is separated from the seed distinguishes the superior rambutan from the inferior ones, for after decades of cross cultivation there is now a wide variety. In the royal courts of Thailand, ladies were specially trained in the art of removing, with a curved knife, all traces of the seed from the pulp and replacing the fruit in its skin, as though untouched.

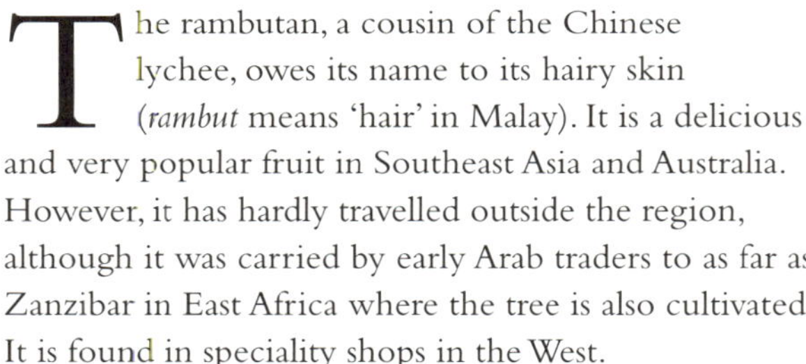

The fruit is also nutritious, with a high vitamin C content. In season it is to be found everywhere, from sophisticated supermarkets—peeled, de-seeded and wrapped in cellophane—to wayside stalls where it is sold in large red bunches, twigs and all. It is best eaten fresh, although its juice and pulp are now canned and exported. Fresh rambutans can be stored for about a week or more in a cool place or if refrigerated.

The rambutan has some traditional medicinal uses, particularly in parts of Indonesia where its rind is dried and used as a medicine.

In Thailand, the fruit is called ngoh, also the name for a curly-haired tribe in the south. A folktale of this country tells of a young girl choosing a husband with a fearful mask and curly hair, knowing he would be kind and handsome—comparing him to the delicious fruit under the not so attractive exterior.

RAMBUTAN TART

Ingredients:

50gm/1/2cup custard powder
25gm/2tbsp cornflour
500ml/2cups milk
150gm/3/4cup sugar
50gm/1cup desiccated coconut
500gm/2 cups rambutan flesh
15gm/1tbsp butter
1 baked tart case
225ml/1cup persimmon pulp
250ml/1cup whipped cream

Method: Mix custard powder and cornflour with 100 ml of milk and stir until smooth. Heat remaining milk, desiccated coconut, sugar and fruit and bring to a boil. Add custard mixture and simmer for 3 minutes stirring continuously. Remove from heat, add butter. Cool and pour into tart case. Before serving, cover tart with a mixture of persimmon pulp and whipped cream.

The attractive appearance of the ruby red fruit with its green and red spikes makes it greatly in demand as a decoration piece—either in a bowl of fruit or with an arrangement of dried flowers.

DIMENSIONS:
fruit:
diameter: 5 cm
length: 7.5 cm
weight: 60–100 gm

SEASON:
all year round

PRODUCTIVITY:
3–5 years

PROPAGATION:
seeds, cuttings

CULINARY USES:
fruit eaten raw; juice taken as drink

Passiflora edulis

PASSION FRUIT

(Thai name: *ka-tok-rok/sao-wa-rot*)

Origin:
Brazil

Distribution:
Tropical lowlands

Varieties:
Yellow and purple

The spectacular flowers with a strong aroma have five stamens shielded by a ring of long, drooping, purple-white 'whiskers' and crowned by pale green canopies.

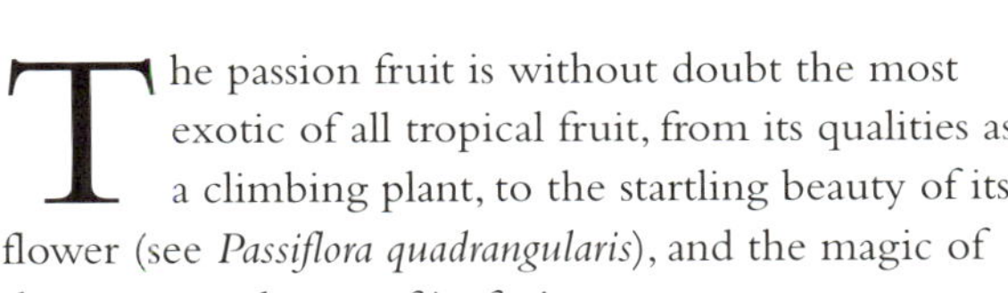

The passion fruit is without doubt the most exotic of all tropical fruit, from its qualities as a climbing plant, to the startling beauty of its flower (see *Passiflora quadrangularis*), and the magic of the aroma and taste of its fruit.

Pride of place, by general consensus, goes to the deep purple *P. edulis*. Another variety of this species has the yellow fruit. Both are green when unripe.

Since the 18th century the passion fruit has been found in many tropical areas outside its native Brazil. The purple species goes under a number of different names, including *granadilla* in Spanish; *maracuja peroba* in Portugese; *lilikoi* in Hawaii; *grenadille* or *couzou* in French and *linmangkon* in Thailand.

The fruit itself has the shape of a large egg and is deep purple or yellow. The skin is thick, tough, smooth and waxy. When ripe, the outer skin dries and shrivels up. The cavity within contains an aromatic mass of membranous sacs filled with an orange coloured pulpy liquid and up to 250 tiny, hard, black-pitted seeds. Most passion fruit lovers do not bother to remove the edible seeds. To obtain the maximum passion fruit juice without getting the seeds: take 10 fruit and after cutting off the tops, scoop the pulp into a bowl. Rub through a sieve, obtaining the extract without seeds. Add the seeds and pulp left over on the sieve to 1/2 a cup of boiling water and cover and let stand for a few minutes. Strain through a cheesecloth, squeezing gently to extract every drop of juice. The resultant juice, which is in the form of a rich, natural extract, can be diluted with water or fruit juices and mixed with sugar to form a refreshing drink. As a flavouring, it can be added to ice creams, soufflés, sauces and yogurt. Surplus juice can be covered and kept refrigerated.

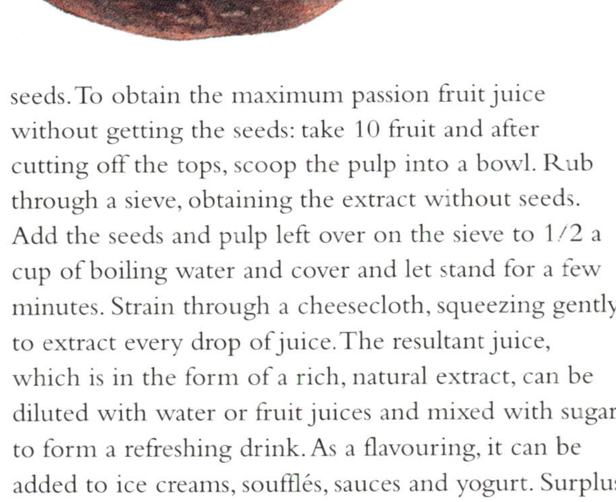

The pharmaceutical industry in Europe has shown a revival of interest in the use of passiflorine, a glycoside, as a sedative. In Brazil, passion fruit juice is given as a digestive stimulant and for the treatment of other gastric ailments. Passion fruit has a very high fibre content if eaten without removing the seeds.

The rind of the fruit is chopped, dried and combined with molasses as cattle or pig fodder. The roots, stem and leaves are poisonous.

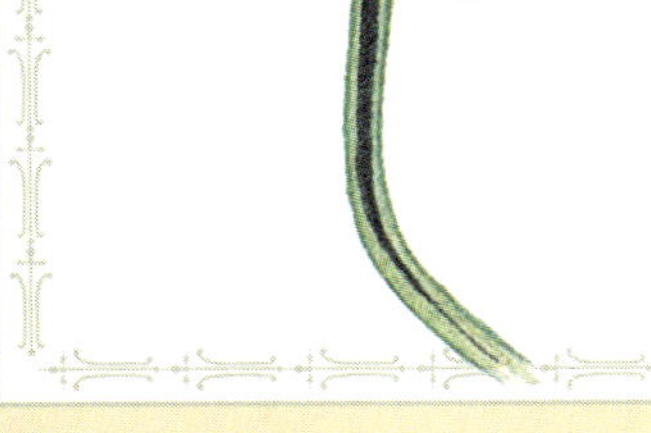

PASSION FRUIT CHARLOTTE

Ingredients:

100gm/3-1/2oz chocolate sponge cake
200gm/40 sponge cake fingers
125ml/1/2cup passion fruit pulp
80gm/2/5cup sugar
15gm/15 gelatine leaves
200ml/4/5cup whipping cream
10ml/2tsp Grand Marnier

Passion fruit gel

50ml/4tbsp passion fruit juice
5gm/2tsp passion fruit seed
3gm/3 gelatine leaves
5gm/1tsp sugar

Method: Line ring cake tin with sliced chocolate cake on the base and finger cake on the sides. Soak cake with Grand Marnier. Place remaining chocolate cake in the middle. Heat passion fruit purée with sugar and add gelatine (dissolved by soaking in water). Cool, and fold in whipped cream. Pour in around the chocolate cake. Top with passion fruit gel.

Courtesy of *Ramada Bintang Bali Resort*

DIMENSIONS:
fruit:
diameter: 20–25 cm
weight: 1–2 kg

SEASON:
all year round

PROPAGATION:
seeds, cuttings

CULINARY USES:
a dessert fruit; canned juice

Passiflora quadrangularis

GIANT GRANADILLA

Origin:
Brazil

Distribution:
Tropical lowlands

Varieties:
Numerous, though only a few are cultivated for fresh consumption as well as for processing

The giant granadilla is one of the most distinguished members of the large passion flower family (Passifloraceae) of tendril-bearing herbaceous vines. The name of this genus may, indeed, suggest love but it actually stands for suffering. The Roman Catholic Spanish missionaries who first came across to the Americas saw in this complex and beautiful flower the symbol of the suffering and agony of Jesus Christ on the cross and named it accordingly.

The leaves which are shiny and have a 'quilting' effect on the surface, formed by the veins, are poisonous. The solitary, white flowers, tinged with pink and violet, are renowned for their spectacular beauty and strong fragrance. The fruit is large, oblong, and has a delicate scent. The skin is smooth, greenish-yellow and has faint, lengthwise ridges on it.

When ripe, the fruit is popularly eaten fresh as a dessert, although sometimes it is taken raw and boiled or cooked as a vegetable. Juice from its pulp makes an excellent drink and in the American tropics it is canned for export.

'Granadilla' means 'little pomegranate'. Reference is obviously to the number of seeds in the fruit.

The beautiful blossoms of the Passifloraceae family, and of the passion flower in particular, are often used to symbolize events in the last hours of the life of Jesus Christ—Passion of Christ—which accounts for the name of this group. The corona is said to represent the crown of thorns, the styles represent the five wounds, and the five sepals and five petals represent 10 of the apostles, excluding Judas, who betrayed Jesus, and Peter, who denied knowing him three times on the night of his trial, thereby fulfilling Jesus' prophecy that Peter would 'betray him three times before the cock crows'.

Persea americana

AVOCADO

(Thai name: *a-vo-ca-do*)

Origin:
Central America

Distribution:
Tropics and subtropics

Varieties:
Several, based on differences of colour, texture, shape and seed size

DIMENSIONS:
tree:
height: up to 40 m
fruit:
length: 7–20 cm,
diameter: 4.5-6 cm,
weight: 0.2-1 kg

SEASON:
fruits twice a year

PRODUCTIVITY:
up to 30 years

PROPAGATION:
seeds, grafting

CULINARY USES:
eaten fresh, as a salad or made into an ice cream

OTHER USES:
oil used in cosmetics and skin care products

In Mexico, mashed avocado is the principal ingredient of guacamole, a characteristic sauce in Mexican cuisine.

The weight of the seed in many varieties accounts for perhaps half the weight of the fruit. Yet the seed is held loosely inside and rattles when the fruit is shaken.

This is the aristocrat of all tropical fruits. Its creamy, yellowish-green flesh, which has the consistency of butter, is rich in iron and potassium, and in vitamins A and B, and has the highest protein content of any fruit in the world. The sheer opulence of the avocado as a food has led to its being treated as an aphrodisiac in certain cultures.

The avocado is shaped like a pear and has a skin resembling that of an alligator, from which it derives the name alligator pear. Like many tropical fruit, the avocado continues to ripen after having been plucked from the tree. When ready for eating, its smooth, shiny skin loses its tautness and changes from yellowish-green to dark green or almost black.

The name 'avocado' is believed to be the Spanish corruption of the Aztec word *ahuacatl*. The plant was long known and cultivated by the Aztec and Mayan of Central America. (Archaeologists have found remnants of seeds dating back to 8,000 BC.) In mid-15th century, the Inca introduced the avocado tree to Peru. Spanish conquistadors who arrived in Mexico and Peru in the 16th century found the fruit growing in abundance. They introduced it to other parts of the tropical world, where it continues to flourish in many variant forms.

The avocado is considered—usually with a degree of elegance—as nature's gift to the busy hostess. Its versatility allows it to be served in many variations, the most commonly found one being with vinaigrette. It can also be added to other dishes to give a certain zest—cubed with chicken or turkey salad; mashed to provide a topping for baked potatoes; a creamy texture to a salad dressing; a stuffing for mushroom caps and omelettes; a topping on a California-style pizza and a filling in sandwiches. A medium avocado will produce about one cup of mashed fruit.

The oil of the avocado is known to be beneficial for the skin. It is used extensively for skin care products by the cosmetics industry in the manufacture of soaps, facial creams and moisturizers.

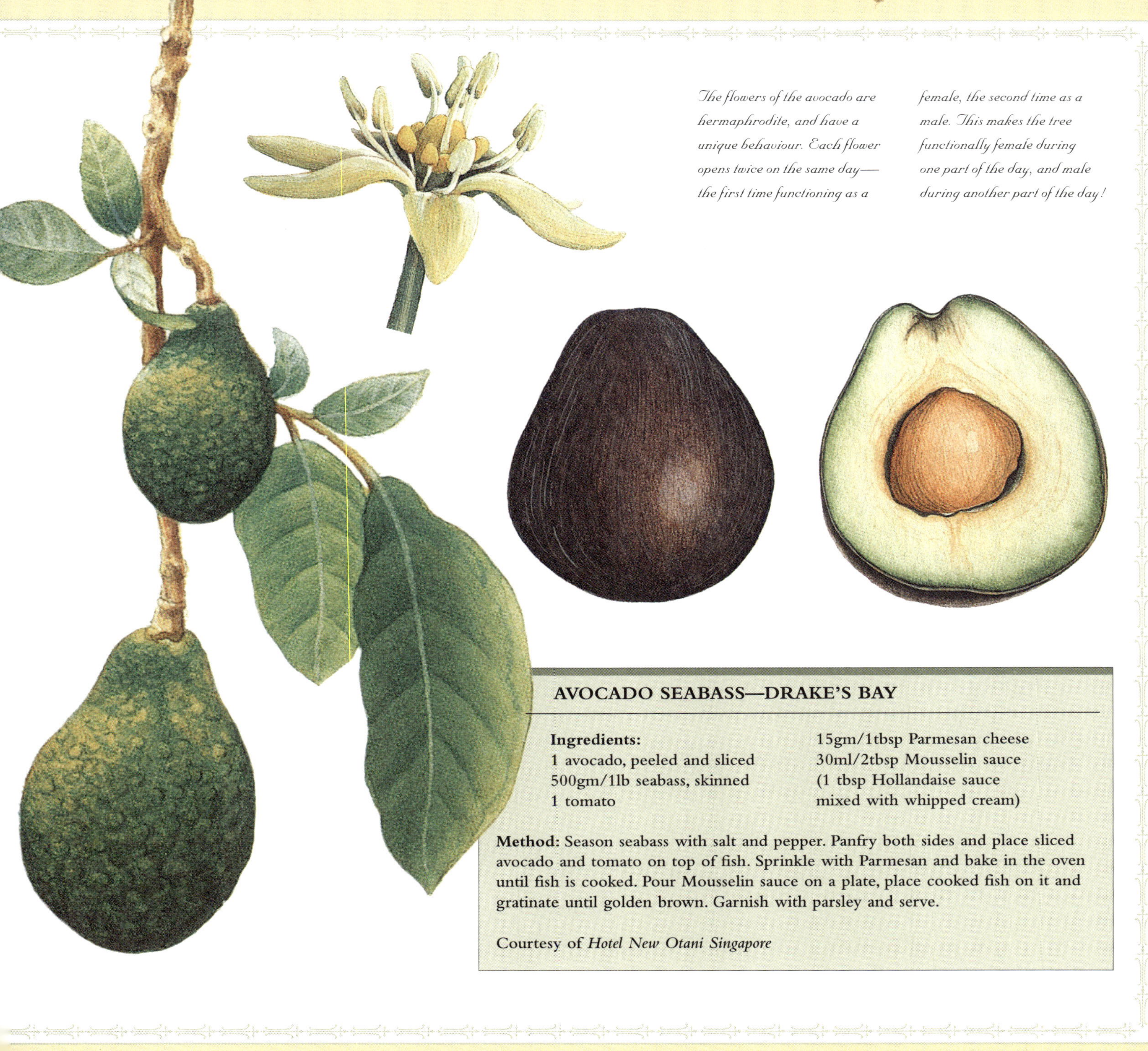

The flowers of the avocado are hermaphrodite, and have a unique behaviour. Each flower opens twice on the same day—the first time functioning as a female, the second time as a male. This makes the tree functionally female during one part of the day, and male during another part of the day!

AVOCADO SEABASS—DRAKE'S BAY

Ingredients:
1 avocado, peeled and sliced
500gm/1lb seabass, skinned
1 tomato
15gm/1tbsp Parmesan cheese
30ml/2tbsp Mousselin sauce
(1 tbsp Hollandaise sauce mixed with whipped cream)

Method: Season seabass with salt and pepper. Panfry both sides and place sliced avocado and tomato on top of fish. Sprinkle with Parmesan and bake in the oven until fish is cooked. Pour Mousselin sauce on a plate, place cooked fish on it and gratinate until golden brown. Garnish with parsley and serve.

Courtesy of *Hotel New Otani Singapore*

DIMENSIONS:
tree:
height: up to 8 m
fruit:
diameter: 2–15 cm
weight: 10 gm–1 kg

SEASON:
all the year round

PRODUCTIVITY:
20–30 years

PROPAGATION:
seeds, cuttings, budding, marcotting.

CULINARY USES:
usually eaten raw, juice as a drink, a seasoning

OTHER USES:
medicinal

Psidium guajava

GUAVA

(Thai name: *fa-rung)*

Origin:
Tropical America

Distribution:
Tropics and warmer subtropics

Varieties:
Some 150—with seeds and seedless and ranging greatly in size and taste

This is a multipurpose tropical fruit with a Spanish name, probably from its native Latin American source, though in this instance its greatest versatility lies in the kitchen. Originating in the tropical Americas (probably Brazil), this hardy and easily cultivated tree is now found throughout the tropical world, where it goes under a host of different names. It was probably spread eastwards by the Portuguese who planted it in their colonies in South-east Asia, including Malaysia and India, as one of its Malay names, *jambu portugis,* suggests. The true Malaysian *jambu,* incidentally, belongs to a different but related family. It was the Spaniards who introduced the guava to the Philippines at an early date.

The guava, with its strong, rich aroma, is a large berry. With a skin that is usually pale yellow or yellowish-green when ripe, the sandy textured flesh can be either creamy-white or salmon-pink, depending upon the variety. The fruit may be almost seedless or packed with numerous tiny, hard seeds which are edible. The taste is sweetish-sour.

As a food source, the guava is particularly gifted, being rich in vitamin C, and also has a high content of vitamin A, iron, potassium and calcium. It is low in sodium and calories. It also has a high pectin content, making it an useful setting agent for jams and jellies. In the tropics, the guava plays the kind of role in pies and pastries that apples do in temperate climates, and lends its flavour easily to ice creams and iced drinks and for use in salads and vegetable dishes. Its juice is canned.

In India, guava leaves are used to treat wounds and also as an antidote to toothache. The Filipinos make a decoction from its leaves and roots to apply to swollen gums, and the fruit is also recommended for acute throat inflammation. Cooked to a thick paste, it is effective in healing boils, sores, ulcers and open wounds.

The bark is used for silk dyes and for tanning, and the wood itself makes excellent firewood.

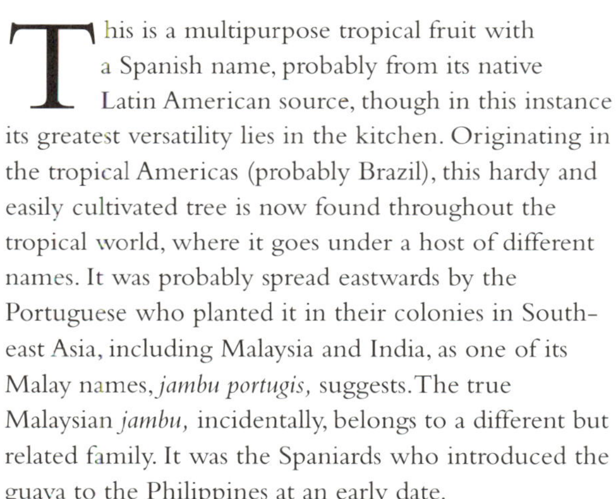

Guava purée freezes well. Cut a washed fruit after removing the blossom end. Purée in a blender. Sieve and freeze in individual ice-cube containers or trays.

MINESTRONE OF FRUITS AND BERRIES WITH GUAVA ESSENCE AND GUAVA SORBET

Minestrone soup
Ingredients:
1 litre/4 cups water
175gm/3/4 cup castor sugar
2tbsp/zest of 2 limes
2 vanilla stick or beans, split
375ml/1 1/2 cups pink guava purée
20gm/2tbsp raspberry purée
10gm/2 1/2tbsp fresh basil leaves

Method: Bring all ingredients to a boil and simmer for 5 minutes. Strain and cool on ice. Keep chilled.

Cocoa grain lacy biscuit
Ingredients:
100gm/3 1/2 cup butter
100gm/5/8cup icing sugar
170ml/1/2cup liquid glucose
100gm/2/3cup cake flour
100gm/2/3cup cocoa powder

Method: Mix all the ingredients into a paste.
Pipe 2–3 cm 'coins' on to waxed paper or a greased dish. Bake at 200°C.

Pink guava sorbet
525ml/2cups pink guava purée
100gm/1/2cup castor sugar
250ml/1/2cup water
35gm/1 1/2tbsp glucose

Method: Heat water, sugar and glucose and bring to a boil. Add purée. Return to fire and cook for a few minutes, stirring continuously, till thick. Remove from fire and cool immediately. Churn in blender and freeze.

To serve
Cut assorted fruit such as kiwi, mango, strawberries, peach and banana. Place in soup plate. Pour chilled soup to cover fruit. Garnish with fresh basil leaves. Scoop Guava Sorbet on top of fruit. Garnish with Cocoa Grain Lacy Biscuit and serve.

Courtesy of *Four Seasons Hotel, Singapore*

Traditional Chinese food therapy recommends guava for diabetes. Take 90gm of fruit, crush and squeeze to obtain the juice. Drink this three times a day, before meals.

DIMENSIONS:
tree:
height: up to 5 m
fruit
diameter: 6–12 cm
weight: 100–300 gm

PRODUCTIVITY:
15–20 years

PROPAGATION:
seeds, cuttings, marcotting

CULINARY USES:
taken fresh; fruit juice and syrup

OTHER USES:
medicinal; ornamental (flower)

The bright red blossom of the pomegranate tree has always been considered a symbol of love and its fruit symbolizes fertility. History has it that the exquisitely beautiful beloved of Prince Salim (who was later crowned Emperor Jahangir and ruled India in the early 17th century) was called Anarkali (Anar—pomegranate; kali—flower bud). She was believed to have been buried alive because the prince's father, Moghul Emperor Akbar, disapproved of his son's love affair with the court dancer.

Punica granatum

POMEGRANATE

(Thai name: *tub-tim)*

Origin:
West Asia (Iran), Eastern Mediterranean

Distribution:
Subtropics (semi-arid); cooler tropics up to 600 m

Varieties:
Several, based on colour

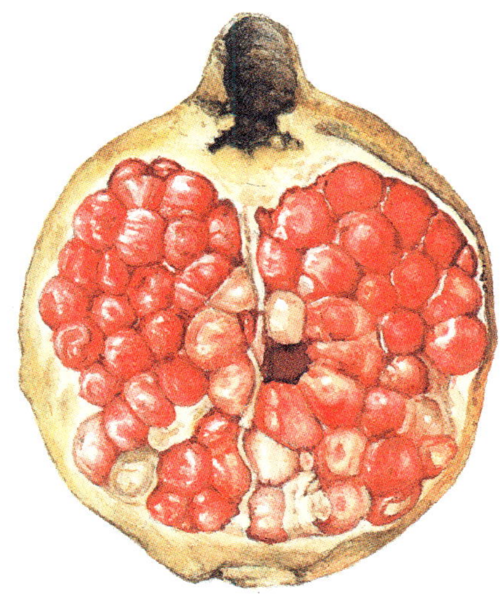

A tropical fruit rich in historical associations, the pomegranate has been cultivated in its West Asian and North African homeland for over 5,000 years and has entered the lore of the region. It appears on the bas-reliefs of ancient Egyptian temples, and was amongst the fruits found in the hanging gardens of Babylon. It was used by Pluto, the lord of the underworld, Hades, in Greek mythology, to seduce the beautiful Persephone. The Romans received it from the Phoenicians (of Lebanon) and hence *Punica,* its scientific name. The Prophet Mohammed recommended the pomegranate as a means to purge the system of envy and hatred. In Chinese, Hebrew, Greek and Roman lore it is regarded as a symbol of fertility and prosperity, and among the Javanese it was associated with certain pregnancy rites. The pomegranate tree features in the Spanish coat of arms, and it is also said to have given its name to the Moorish kingdom of Granada in Spain.

Whether the appeal of the pomegranate lay in the conspicuous beauty of its brilliant red flowers or in the dark pink juicy pulp found contained within its tough smooth exterior must remain a moot point, but it was carried to other parts of the tropical world from its starting point by early Arab, Persian and Indian traders, its hard skin making it a good traveller.

The scarlet fruit pulp envelops numerous small, crunchy white seeds, which are also edible but are not to everybody's taste. It is this abundance of seeds that gives the fruit its name, derived from the Latin *pomum granatum* which translates as 'fruit with many seeds'.

The somewhat astringent juice is an excellent thirst-quencher and can be made into a fine syrup. The fruit also finds a great range of applications in icings, salad dressings, soups and puddings and can be used to flavour sauces and pickles.

The pomegranate has several uses in traditional medicine, including as a gargle for persistent coughs, as an antidote for fevers, for diarrhoea and colic and to remove intestinal worms in children. This is because the rind of the fruit is astringent and contains a certain amount of poison. Ancient Egyptians made wine from it, with the flavour of raspberry, which may or may not have been good for their health.

ROASTED DUCK BREAST WITH MANGO SALSA AND MESCLUN GREENS IN POMEGRANATE VINAIGRETTE

Roasted Duck Breast
Ingredients:
140gm/1 duck breast fillet
1/4tsp each thyme/rosemary
salt and pepper to taste
100gm/3-1/2oz boiled, skinned potatoes

Method: Season duck with herbs, salt and pepper and sear on a hot pan on all sides. Roast duck in preheated oven at 400°F for 20 minutes. Cool and slice.

Mesclun Green Salad
30gm/1cup mesclun (mix of rocket, mache, oak leaf lettuce, curly endive, chervil) greens
1 wonton skin

Method: To prepare wonton basket, heat oil in a wok, deep-fry wonton skin. Using a ladle press convex side onto the skin. Remove from oil when golden. Cool. Place greens in basket.

Pomegranate Vinaigrette
50gm/1/2cup pomegranate seeds
20gm/1tbsp chopped shallot
5gm/1tsp chopped chervil
juice of one lemon
60ml/1/4cup champagne vinegar
60ml/1/4cup olive oil
1/2tsp sugar

Method: Combine all ingredients and mix well.

Mango Salsa
Ingredients:
20gm/2tbsp diced ripe mango
5gm/1tsp chopped red onion
2gm/1tbsp coriander leaves
30ml/2tbsp olive oil
juice of 1/2 lemon

Method: Combine all ingredients.

To serve: Lay sliced potato and duck in the centre of a plate, with salsa on the side. Pour vinaigrette over greens in wonton basket and set on side of plate.

Courtesy of *The Oriental Singapore*

The pomegranate features as a symbol of love in many romances: Romeo's nightingale serenaded Juliet under this beautiful tree.

Aphrodite, the Greek goddess of beauty and love, was said to have planted the first pomegranate tree.

DIMENSIONS:
tree:
height: up to 7 m
fruit:
diameter: 2.5 cm
weightof bunch: 2–3 kg

SEASON
all year round

PRODUCTIVITY:
15–20 years

PROPAGATION:
seeding, marcotting of ratoons (new shoots after cropping)

CULINARY USES:
eaten as fresh fruit

OTHER USES:
matting (from stems)

In different parts of Southeast Asia the fresh fruit are candied, pickled and used in a salad.

Salacca zalacca

SNAKEFRUIT

(Thai name: *sa-la/ra-kum)*

Origin:
Indonesia

Distribution:
Southeast Asian lowlands up to 500 m

Known as *salak* in Indonesia and Malaysia, this is an Indonesian fruit par excellence—hardly known outside that country, but very popular amongst Indonesians, and in the markets of neighbouring Thailand and Malaysia where it is grown on a small scale. It is also being exported to the European markets. Its failure to attract a much larger, global patronage may well be because of its English name, suggested by the snake-like appearance of its scaly, thin brown skin.

The salak palm is virtually trunkless, with both the spiny fronds and the fruit bunches emerging at ground level. Each bunch contains 10–20 fruit, each of which has three segments. In some, all three are fully developed with a seed. Other fruit may have one or two immature, seedless segments. The male and female flowers are found on separate plants, with the latter being larger than the former.

Despite its sinister appearance and fierce protective shield, the fruit is nutritious, which accounts for its local popularity. Its flesh is firm, yet soft and translucent, and when ripe, tastes like a blend of pineapple and banana. The mature palm bears between 30 and 300 fruit. The inedible seed within is round, brownish black with a very hard testa, which cracks easily when dried, especially in some sweet and juicy varieties.

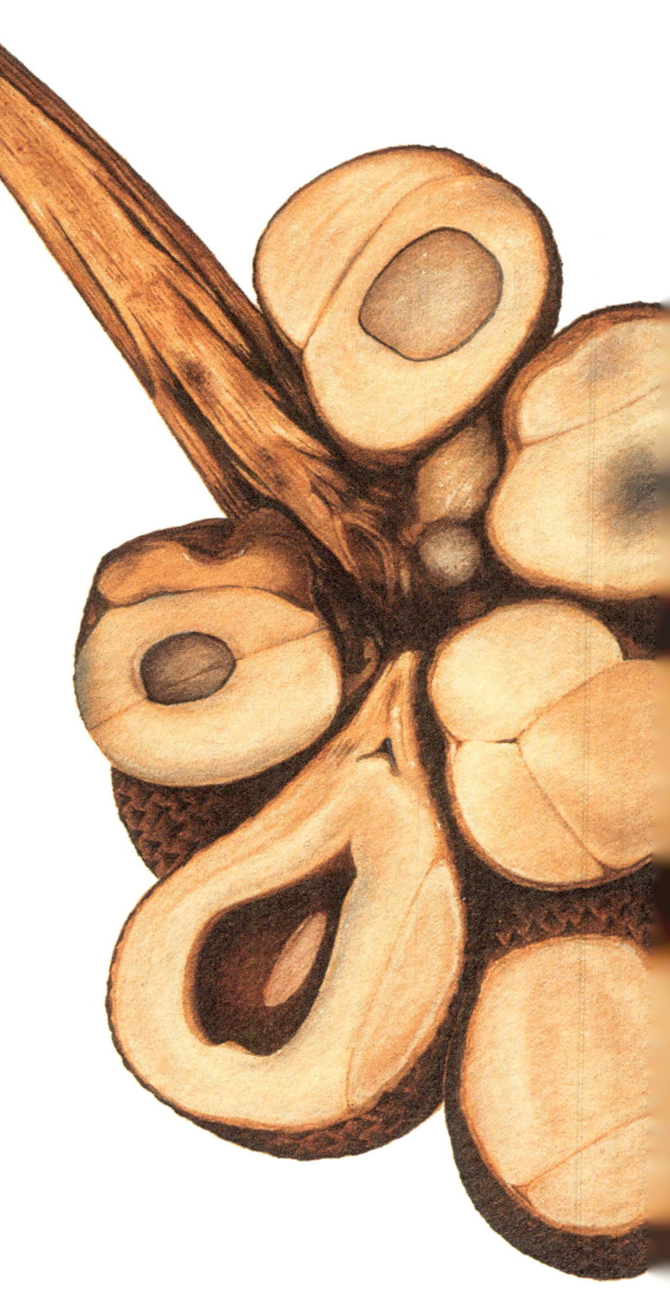

SNAKEFRUIT COMPOTE

Ingredients:
500gm/1lb snakefruit with shell removed
100gm/1/2cup sugar
1.5l/6cups water

Method: Boil water. Add sugar and dissolve. Add washed snakefruit and cook till tender. Remove, cool, peel skin and de-seed. Serve chilled.

Courtesy of *The Ritz-Carlton Bali*

Newly harvested fruit are best kept in a ventilated container, usually a bamboo basket or loosely woven mat. Good quality, undamaged fruit can be kept for up to two months. Damaged or rotting fruit must be quickly separated to reduce the risk of affecting the remaining crop.

The fruit, also called 'dragon's eggs', is covered with regularly arranged scales, giving it the appearance of a small prickly pine cone. In the ripe fruit a layer of granular-looking flesh adheres to the kernel; whereas each kernel of an immature fruit lies free in a cavity in the flesh.

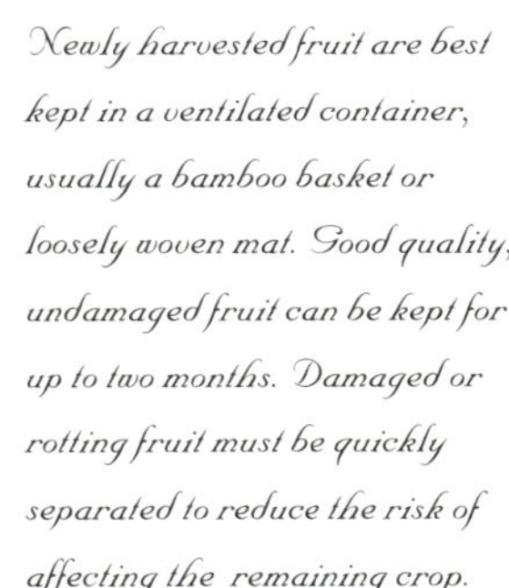

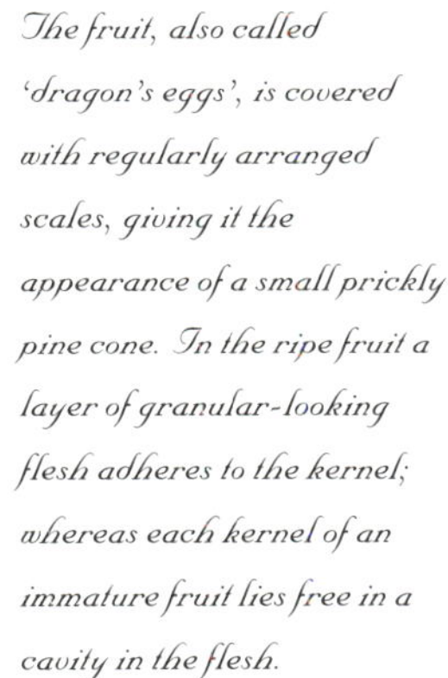

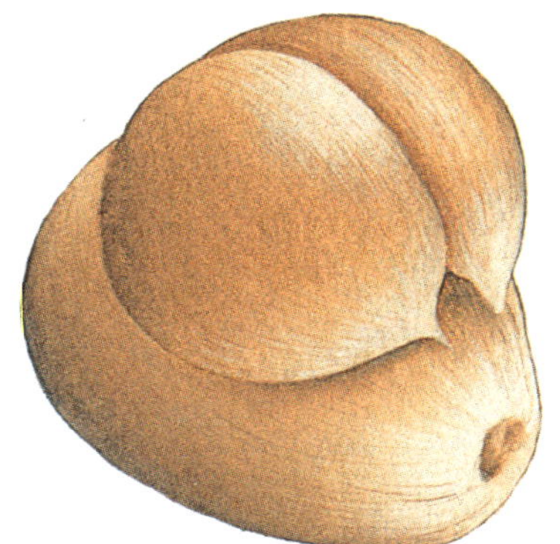

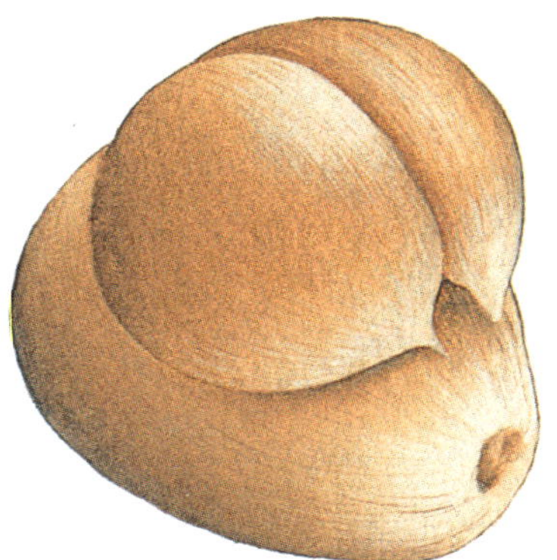

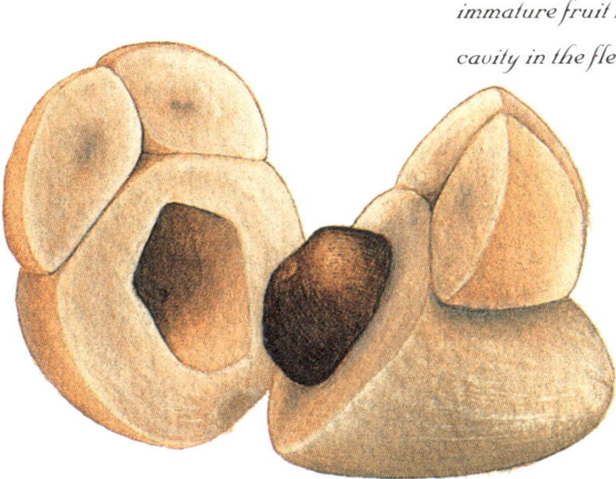

DIMENSIONS:
tree: height: up to 18 m
fruit: diameter: 5–8 cm
SEASON: several harvests a year
PROPAGATION: marcotting
CULINARY USES: eaten fresh or cooked in jam
OTHER USES: medicinal

Syzygium malaccensis

MALAY APPLE

(Thai name: *chom-poo)*

Origin:
Indonesia and Malaysia

Distribution:
Indonesia, Thailand and Peninsular Malaysia

Varieties:
Various, based on colour and/or shape

The Malay apple must have spread throughout the islands of the Pacific in very early times for it is featured in Fijian mythology. The wood was used by the Hawaiians to make idols in ancient times, and it has been recorded that before the arrival of missionaries in Hawaii there were no fruits on the islands except bananas, coconuts and the Malay apple.

The showy, pink to deep red flowers which tend to remain hidden by the the tree's thick foliage until they fall, forming a lovely carpet on the ground, were considered sacred to Pele, the fiery goddess of volcanoes in Hawaii.

The Malay apple is admired as much for the flavour of its fruit as it is for the beauty of its tree, its vibrant, deep red flowers and crimson fruit. Called *jambu bol* or *jambu merah* locally, it is the Malaysian and Indonesian representative of the grand, worldwide myrtle and eucalyptus family. Its closest cousins are the water apple (*jambu air*) and rose apple (*jambu mawar*); *jambu* is the generic Malay term for this local branch of the family.

Opinions are divided as to the relative merits of the edible jambu fruit, but for many the Malay apple reigns supreme. It is certainly the largest of them all. It is bell-shaped and has a smooth, waxy skin that is delicate enough to be eaten, ripening from green to an attractive, rich rose-red or crimson.

Because the skin is so delicate, the fruit is easily bruised and so is rarely seen for sale in the market. Instead, it is found in gardens and orchards where it is consumed on the spot. It does not have a strong flavour, but it is juicy and refreshing.

The Malay apple is found in most tropical regions, where rainfall is plentiful and perennial. It was carried by the Portuguese conquerors of Melaka to Goa, and from Goa by Arab and Indian traders to West Africa, and eventually found its way to the West Indies.

In 1793, Captain Bligh is said to have carried small trees of three varieties to Jamaica from the islands of Timor and Tahiti. The Malay apple is believed to have been one of them.

The timber of the Malay apple tree is hard, but not suitable for practical purposes. Its fruit, leaves and roots are used in traditional medicine. The Malays make a preparation of the root to use for itches. Cracks in the tongue are treated with the powder of dried leaves. In Cambodia, the Malay apple is used to treat fevers and the root is used for oedema and as a diuretic. In Brazil, constipation, diabetes, headaches, pulmonary complaints and coughs are treated effectively by various parts of the plant. The fruit, seeds, bark and leaves, due to their antibiotic qualities, are known to be effective for ailments of the respiratory system and for high blood pressure. The juice extracted from fresh leaves is applied either as a lotion to soften the skin or added to bath water for the same effect.

In Puerto Rico, both red and white table wines are made. Pick the fruit as soon as they are fully coloured. Dip in boiling water for a minute to destroy surface bacteria. Remove the seeds, blend the fruit and weigh the pulp. Add twice the amount of water, and 680 gm (1-1/2 lbs) of sugar per gallon. Pour the mixture into a sterilized barrel covered with cheese-cloth. Add yeast and insert a coil to stir the mixture. Keep barrel in the coolest part of the house for six months to a year. Filter the pale-rose wine. Add red food colour if desired.

For white wine, no water is added. Peel fruit and blend. Add 565 gm (1-1/4 lbs) sugar per gallon pulp. Ferment for 3 to 6 months.

DIMENSIONS:

tree:
height: 20–30 m

fruit:
diameter: 2–3 cm
length: 5–10 cm

SEASON:
in the dry season

PROPAGATION:
seeds; marcotting

CULINARY USES:
jam; syrup; chutney; pickle; for use in confectionery; flour (from seeds)

OTHER USES:
medicinal; metal cleanser

Superstitions surround the ornamental tamarind:
** In certain parts of India, Hindus marry a tamarind tree to a mango tree before eating the fruit of the latter.*
** It is the dwelling place of the rain-god, according to the Burmese.*
** In Malawi, a paste of tamarind bark and corn is fed to domestic fowls in the belief that if they stray or are stolen, it will help them find their way home.*
** It is considered unhealthy to sleep under this tree because of the falling leaves' high acid content, and because at night the leaves 'exhale acid'.*

Tamarindus indica

TAMARIND

(Thai name: *ma-kharm*)

Origin:
Tropical Africa

Distribution:
Throughout the tropics in less humid areas

Varieties:
Sweet and sour, but mostly sour

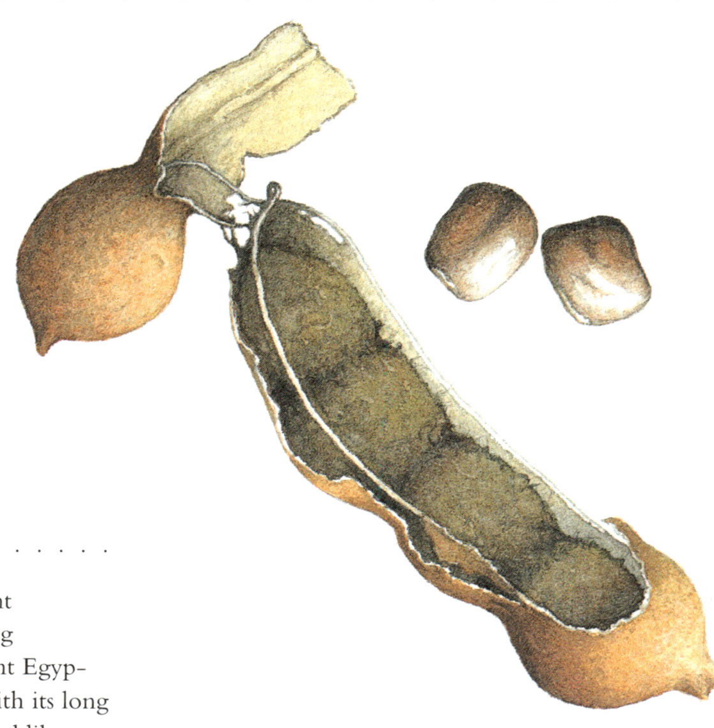

The tamarind, which is of very ancient lineage among cultivated fruits, being known amongst others to the ancient Egyptians, really belongs to the vegetable order, with its long bean-like pods and seeds. However, it is treated like a fruit. Its name is derived from the Arabic *tamar,* meaning a dry date fruit, applied in this instance to an Indian ('Hind') setting. It was Arabs in India who gave the name of 'tamar-hindi' to this tree.

The pod is green at the immature stage. As it matures, it becomes fatter and changes colour to a sandy brown. The flesh of the fruit consists of dry, sticky, dark brown pulp covering, and between, the shiny black seeds in its pod, and tastes like 'hot, unsweetened lemon'. There are a few thick strands, running along the length of the pod, which seemingly enclose the pulp. Its high tartaric acid content, together with an even greater amount of sugar, accounts for the relative sourness and sweetness of different varieties according to the balance between them. But the preferred type is the sour tamarind which provides the favourite flavouring for a host of fish and curry dishes.

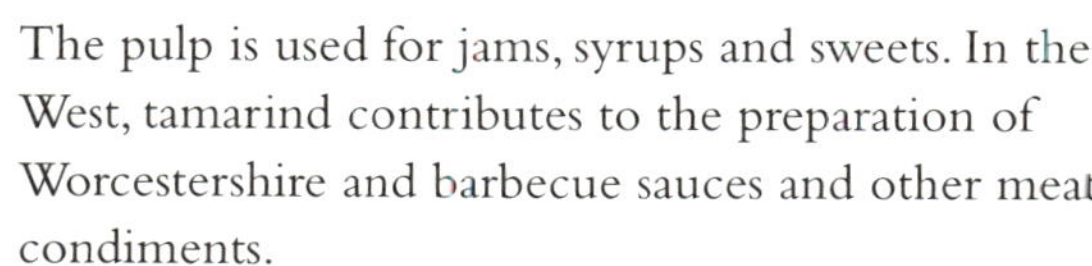

The pulp is used for jams, syrups and sweets. In the West, tamarind contributes to the preparation of Worcestershire and barbecue sauces and other meat condiments.

Rich in vitamin C, the medicinal uses of tamarind are uncountable. Its usefulness as a laxative and in fever cures is universally known. The pulp, leaves and flowers, in various combinations, are applied on painful and swollen joints. It is used as a gargle for sore throats, and as a drink to bring relief from sunstroke. Its bark, in various preparations, is a traditional remedy for sores, ulcers, and boils. Its heated juice is used to cure conjunctivitis, and in Malaysia and Thailand it is given as a medicament to elephants, not merely to cure their aches and pains but also to make them wiser!

Finally, tamarind juice is a great cleanser of brass, copper and other metals.

In the Bahamas, a great delicacy is the fully-grown but yet unripe tamarind pods, called 'swells'. They are roasted in hot coals until they burst. The skin is then peeled back and the sizzling pulp dipped into the ashes and eaten.

Tamarind beverages are quite popular in the tropics. For a simple homemade drink, shell the fruit and place 3-4 pods (or more, if you want a stronger concoction) in a bottle of water. Let it stand for a few hours. Add one tablespoonful or more of sugar and shake. Strain. Add seasonings such as ginger, pepper, cloves and cinnamon. Dilute with chilled water and serve.

TAMARIND SORBET

Ingredients:

300gm/1cup tamarind pulp, cleaned and de-seeded
160gm/3/4cup white sugar
80gm/1/2cup brown sugar, lightly packed
1 egg white, lightly whisked
550ml/scant pint water

Method: Prepare tamarind juice by boiling 300 ml water with tamarind pulp for about 10 minutes. Strain. Combine the resulting juice with the remaining water in a saucepan. Add both sugars and boil for 5 minutes. Remove from fire and cool. Fold in egg white. Put mixture in an blender or in a bowl, and freeze partially for approximately 20 minutes before serving. Makes approximately 1 litre sorbet.
Courtesy of *The Ritz-Carlton Bali*

Practical Tips

Drying fruit:

Judging by the range of dried fruit available in the supermarket, it is obviously a very popular snack food, especially among children. And it is certainly more nutritious than sweets or chocolates!

The other uses for dried fruit are in baking and cooking. The traditional method of drying fruit out in the sun is giving way to the more practical oven-dried variety in the kitchen. Dried properly, fruit keep their flavour for up to six months if stored in airtight containers and refrigerated.

Dried fruit are higher in calories, sugar, and fibre than fresh fruit because the water content evaporates and the flesh and skin darken and the sugar content is concentrated.

To oven-dry fruit:

- Select firm, bruise-free fruit. Wash, peel, core and cut into 5 mm (1/4") slices.
- Lay fruit in a single layer on wax paper or a baking dish, cut size facing up. Put in a warm oven at 140°F/60°C for about six hours.
- Remove from the oven and lay the fruit on the kitchen counter and let dry in the open air for a day or so, turning it over occasionally.
- The fruit is ready when it is wrinkled and has shrunk to 3/4 of its original size and there is a slight change in colour. At the same time, it must be soft and juicy.

When cooking with fruit:

- When using dried food in cooking, soak the fruit—at room temperature—in hot water, wine or brandy before use. Unsoaked fruit turns hard during cooking.
- When using fresh fruit for desserts, use ripe or even slightly overripe fruit for best flavour.
- Blending or macerating fruit is best done when the fruit is at room temperature rather than soon after refrigeration.

Extracting juice:

From a pomegranate: While this may sound difficult or impossible, it can be done! Choose a fruit that is heavy, as that means more juice. Roll the pomegranate on a countertop and knead it simultaneously. This crushes the fruit inside and breaks the juice sacs and you can hear the rupturing sound. Once this is done, cut the fruit into half, taking care not to spill the juice (as it can stain the surface). Extract the juice, as you would do with an orange or lemon, using a manual citrus juicer. Strain the juice through a fine sieve. Collect the seeds in a fine cloth and squeeze them to obtain as much juice as possible. Discard the seeds. One large pomegranate (approx. 500 gm) yields 1/2 cup juice).

To ripen fruit:

To ripen fruit faster, wrap them individually in paper or keep them in a covered container along with a ripe apple or banana. Both these fruit give off a gas which hastens ripening.

Sorbet and sherbet:

Sorbet: A French word to describe a smooth-textured, fat-free frozen fruit dish or mixture of wine and a syrup. It may also contain fruit juice, milk, egg whites etc. Derived from the Old Italian *sorbetto*, from the Turkish *serbet*, and the Arabic *sharbah* and Persian *sharbat*.

Sherbet: The American version of sorbet. It is creamier, contains a little milk, light cream, yogurt or egg white which is added to fruit purée. In the mid-eastern countries like Turkey and the Arab nations, and in India and Pakistan, a sherbet is a cooling, refreshing drink made from sweetened fruit juice and even rose petals.

Temperature conversions

To convert Fahrenheit (F) to Celsius (C):

– *32 from the F figure,* **x** *by 5 and ÷ the total by 9.*

–17.7°C = 0°F (freezing point)

100°C = 210°F (boiling point)

0°C = 32°F

37.7°C = 100°F (exact conversion)

–10°F = –25°C (freezer temperature)

140°F to 200°F = 60°C to 95°C (warm oven)

300°F to 350°F = 150°C to 180°C (baking)

375°F to 400°F = 190°C to 200°C (hot oven)

425°F to 450°F = 220°C to 230°C (very hot oven)

475°F to 500°F = 250°C to 260°C (broiling)

175°F/80°C is the correct temperature to keep foods warm at, for serving, without changing their composition or drying out.

CONVERSION CHART

Exact conversion

1 oz = 28.35 gm

For practical purposes, measurements can be converted as follows:

Dry measurements

1 oz = 30 gm	1 pinch = less than 1/8 tsp
2 oz = 60 gm	1 tsp = 1/3 tbsp
3 oz = 90 gm	2 tbsp = 6 tsp
4 oz = 125 gm	1/4 cup = 4 tbsp
5 oz = 150 gm	1/2 cup = 8 tbsp
6 oz = 180 gm	1/3 cup = 5 tbsp+1 tsp
7 oz = 200 gm	2/3 cup = 10 tbsp+2 tsp
8 oz = 250 gm	3/4 cup = 12 tbsp
1 lb = 500 gm	1 cup = 50 tsp
2 lb = 1 kg	1 cup = 16 tbsp

Liquid measurements

1 tbsp = 15 ml

3+1/3 tbsp = 50 ml

6+1/2 tbsp = 100 ml

2/3 cup = 150 ml

1 cup = 250 ml

1+1/4 cups = 300 ml

2 cups = 500 ml

1 pint = 2+1/3 cups = 600 ml

1 quart = 4 cups = 1 l

Two Tropical Fruit Recipes

ROJAK BUAHAN (SPICY TROPICAL FRUIT SALAD)

Ingredients:

Salad:
8 red Malay apple
200gm/1cup ripe pineapple
200gm/1cup half-ripe papaya
400gm/2 half-ripe mangoes
100gm/1 ripe guava

Sambal rojak:
60gm/1/4 cup black shrimp paste
80ml/1/3cup tamarind juice
12gm/1tbsp sugar
15ml/1tbsp lime juice
30gm/2tbsp *sambal* chilli

Sauce:
160gm/2/3cup *sambal rojak*
60gm/1/4cup lukewarm water

Garnish:
16 local lettuce leaves
10gm/2 tsp toasted seasame seeds
4 wanton skins sliced into 1/2cm strips
60ml/4 tbsp cooking oil

Method: *salad and garnish:*
Peel and cut each fruit separately into cubes of about 1 cm. Set aside. Heat the oil in a wok and deep fry the wanton skins until golden brown. Remove and place on an absorbent paper towel to drain off excess oil. Set aside. Arrange lettuce leaves on a plate. Place the diced fruit on the leaves and pour the sauce over the fruit. Garnish with crispy wanton skins. Sprinkle toasted seasame seeds over the salad.

Photograph by Diana Lynn

Method: *Sambal rojak*:
Combine all ingredients and mix well. Make into a sauce with lukewarm water until consistency is smooth.
Serves 4

Courtesy of *Raffles Hotel, Singapore*

FARM CHICKEN, PRAWN AND TROPICAL FRUIT SALAD

Ingredients:
20gm/2tbsp each mango, papaya, and banana, peeled and sliced
6 lychees, peeled and stoned
120gm/4oz chicken breast
4 fresh prawn, blanched
salt and black pepper to taste
coriander sprigs, to garnish
30gm mesclun greens

Mixed salad dressing:
24gm/2tbsp sugar dissolved in
70ml/5 tbsp hot water
juice of 1/2 lime
15ml/1tbsp fish sauce
1gm/1 red chilli, sliced
1 clove garlic, sliced
30ml/2tbsp olive oil

Method: Season the chicken with salt and pepper and bake in hot oven for 15 minutes. Slice finely. Blend all ingredients of salad dressing. In a bowl, mix together the fruits, prawn, chicken and dressing. Transfer to a plate and garnish with coriander.

Courtesy of *Pan Pacific Hotel Singapore*

Bibliography

Books:

Allen, Betty Molesworth (1967), *Malayan Fruits*, Singapore: Donald Moore Press.

----- (1975), *Common Malaysian Fruits*, Kuala Lumpur: Longman Malaysia.

Bacon, Josephine (1988), *Exotic Fruits A–Z*, London: Xanadu Publications.

Bessette, Alan E. and Chapman, William K. (1992), *Plants and Flowers,* New York: Dover Publications.

Chin, H. F. and Yong, H. S. (1982), *Malaysian Fruits in Colour*, Kuala Lumpur: Tropical Press.

Cooper, Wendy (1994), *Fruits of the Rain Forest*, Chatswood: A GEO Production.

Dai, Yin-fang and Liu, Cheng-jun (1999), *Fruits as Medicine*, Kuala Lumpur: Pelanduk Publications.

DeVanna Fish, Kathleen (1997), *The Gardener's Cookbook*, Monterey: Bon Vivant Press.

Eiseman, Fred and Margaret (1988), *Fruits of Bali*, Berkeley: Periplus Editions.

Hutton, Wendy (1996), *Tropical Fruits of Malaysia and Singapore,* Singapore: Periplus Editions.

McHenry, Robert (gen. ed.) (1992), *The New Encyclopædia Britannica*, Chicago: Encyclopædia Britannica, Inc.

Morton, Julia F. (1987), *Fruits of Warm Climates*, Winterville: Creative Resource Systems.

Nathan, Anne and Wong Yit Chee (1987), *A guide to Fruits and Seeds*, Singapore: Singapore Science Centre.

Othman, Yaacob and Subhardabandhu, Suranant (1995), *The Production of Economic Fruits in South-East Asia*, Kuala Lumpur: Oxford University Press.

Page, P. E. (1984), *Tropical Tree Fruits for Australia,* Brisbane: Queensland Department of Primary Industries.

Piper, Jacqueline M. (1989), *Fruits of South-East Asia: Facts and Folklore*, Singapore: Oxford University Press.

Schneider, Elizabeth (1986), *Uncommon Fruits and Vegetables*, New York: Harper and Row.

Tantillo, Tony and Gugino, Sam (1997), *Eat Fresh, Stay Healthy, An A-to-Z Guide to Buying and Cooking Fruits and Vegetables*, New York: Macmillan.

Tirtawinata, Mohamad Reza; Othman, Yaacob; Veevers-Carter, Wendy and Sidharta, Amir (1995), *Fruit of Indonesia,* Jakarta: Taman Buah Mekarsari.

van Nooten, Berthe Hoola (1993), *Flowers, Fruit and Foliage of the Tropics*, Singapore: Sun Tree Publishing.

Verheij, E. W. M and Coronel, R. E. (1992), *Plant Resources of South-East Asia 2*, Bogor, Indonesia, Prosea Foundation.

Yen Ho, Alice (1995), *At the South-East Asian Table*, Kuala Lumpur: Oxford Univeristy Press.

Websites:

http://www.hort.purdue.edu
http://www.ku.ac.th/AgrInfo/fruit/product
http://www.geocities.com/The Tropics/Cabana/ /2277/rare_fruits.html
http://www.proscitech.com.au/trop/c.html
http://www.fruits.com

TAXONOMY—Classification of plants

Modern botanists and naturalists derive their classification from the binomial system devised by the 18th-century Swede, Carl von Linne (Latinized as Linnaeus). The classification was further refined by the early-19th-century French botanist, A. L. de Jussieu. They used both Latin and Greek names which have since constituted the basic language of botany.

The plant kingdom is further subdivided into different taxonomic groups comprising various taxa (singular: taxon)—divisions, classes, orders, families, genera and species. In the hierarchy of plant classification, each taxon consists of more components than the one above it. Species form the largest number of taxa and are grouped into genera which are, in turn, grouped into families and so on, until the division level. Therefore, in the example *Mangifera indica*, '*Mangifera*' is the name of the genus; '*indica*' is the name of the species.

INDEX